Change Wit

MW00931337

As an evolution biologist, I am thrilled that my field increasingly recognizes cooperation as more natural to humans than competition. Thus I find Jane's book very important in its clear "big picture" view of our world and the urgency of our challenge to act and think outside our habitual Darwinian story to experience ourselves in interdependent, cooperative community with others rather than as separate. Urging us to link issues and disciplines, rather than viewing them in isolation, she reveals the inner changes required to gain the profound insights needed to survive as a thriving living system in which individual capacities are woven into collective action.

> —*Elisabet Sahtouris*, evolution biologist, futurist, author (*Earthdance: Living Systems in Evolution*), speaker, consultant in Living Systems Design

This is a book that will help us change the world. It is both wide and deep, far-ranging and far-seeing, like its amazing author, Dr. Jane Battenberg. Jane is a fearless traveler who guides her readers into adventures through history and into the future. She provides stimulating ways and means that incite us to live and serve more beautifully and more effectively. Her book offers an exciting once-in-a-lifetime journey to authentic change—inside and out. You will enjoy the ride!

> —*Peggy Rubin*, author of *To Be and How to Be: Transforming Your Life through the Power of Sacred Theatre*, director of the Center for Sacred Theatre, Ashland, Oregon

Change Within is immediate relief from these dangerous times. Changing *you* changes everything. Jane Battenberg shows you how. Her introduction lays out the landscape of a world crying for change, describing its contours and trigger points. As a writer she moves intuitively and teaches readers to do the same. Flip through her chapters until one touches you. The effects are amazing!

> —*Richard Owen Geer, PhD*, Story Bridge practitioner, coauthor of *Open Circle: Story Arts and The Reinvention of Community*

Jane Battenberg clearly and thoughtfully presents the state of our physical and emotional world within the context of its history, provides the necessary tools for individuals to discover their own source of strength to change their inward and, therefore, outward approach, and firmly insists that we, collectively, use this awareness to move humanity forward. This call-to-(linking)-arms is not just a self-help book, but a universal help book.

> —*N. Bellamy Jones*, Gen X mother, teacher, author

This book is for young people who read thoughtfully and want to engage deeply with ideas and figure out how they pertain to their lives. Dr. Battenberg masterfully surveys the broad landscapes of personal development, transformational psychology, philosophy, and activism, and gives us an accessible and delightful road map for how to apply this huge amount of wisdom to our personal lives. As a young "seeker" who is passionate about bringing my values to the real world in measurable ways, I found in *Change Within, Change the World* answers to many vital questions that I have been asking myself. This book takes New Age wisdom and thinking and breaks them down into practical, how-to steps so that we can go about the necessary work of healing our planet.

> —*Lucy Claire Curran*, Millennial, career coach, artist, writer, and performer

Also by Jane Rigney Battenberg

Coauthored with Martha M. Rigney
Eye Yoga: How you see is how you think

Change Within,
Change the World

Jane Rigney Battenberg, DCH, MA

BALBOA.
PRESS

A DIVISION OF HAY HOUSE

Balboa Press books may be ordered through booksellers or by contacting:

Balboa Press
A Division of Hay House
1663 Liberty Drive
Bloomington, IN 47403
www.balboapress.com
1 (877) 407-4847

Print information available on the last page.

Cover design by Kelly Fujikawa and Align Visual Arts
Photograph of the author © Christopher Briscoe

ISBN: 978-1-9822-1069-4 (sc)
ISBN: 978-1-9822-1070-0 (e)

Library of Congress Control Number: 2018910157

Balboa Press rev. date: 09/17/2018

To Ron Cordek, my husband and soul mate,
who kept encouraging me to write this book.

Contents

Section 3: Developing Skills

Section 4: Creating Personal Change

Section 5: Shifting Perspectives to Enhance Changes

Section 6: Engaging Subtler Resources

Foreword

Late in life, in a letter to John Adams reflecting on the future of the United States, Thomas Jefferson wrote, "Yes, we did produce a near-perfect republic. But will they keep it? Or will they, in the enjoyment of plenty, lose the memory of freedom? Material abundance without character is the path of destruction."

You may rightly ask that with so many shadows and challenges, and with the avalanche of avarice and ignorance accosting us, how can we ever deal with these things in such a way that our higher humanity, our required human, is not compromised? Either we can undergo a progressive deactivation of the conditioned and pathogenic personality wrought by present civilization, the way of the excellent therapist, or we can find the ways and means to the emergence of a more profound awareness in which the experience of *being* and the felt meaning of life have their foundation, and that, in spite of constituting our true nature, lies ordinarily in our so-called civilized condition, in a darkened or veiled condition—as if asleep. Probably it is both/and with regard to the release of old conditions and the discovery of ways into the light. When Sigmund Freud wrote *Civilization and Its Discontents*, I doubt that he had the idea of the dazzling darkness that lies beneath the darkness of civilization. We can learn to wake up and consciously change and, in so doing, find ourselves repatterned to what I have been calling the possible human.

In this splendid exploration of the dynamics of change, the author, after presenting a remarkable overview of the stages of human and cultural development, moves back from her telescopic lens to a microscopic one that uncovers the latent genius of the human condition and how we can deliver ourselves from disaster into life lived faithful to the earth and to each other.

I am not surprised that Jane Battenberg is so prescient and evocative, because she is expert in the most intimate of all lenses, the human eye. Her work and book on *Eye Yoga* is a brilliant and original revelation of new ways of seeing that lead to new ways of being. Now, in this present volume, written with wit and wisdom, she reveals the ways of changing our operating system through a different set of views and manner of viewing. You will be offered methods and practices for living every day with beauty, energy, power, and grace. In the pages to follow, you will find answers to some of life's most important questions and learn to utilize the answers you discover in your everyday life. With Jane Battenberg as your guide, the work you will do together will be stimulating, depth sourcing, soul charging, and always, celebratory.

This is a rare and very wise book by a rare and wise woman. With mastery and deep intelligence, she leads you on a thrilling journey to the domains of latent potentials and human possibility. Herein you experience redevelopment with potent and evocative exercises that charge your spirit as they change your body, mind, and life.

For indeed, this is a field book to creating the next stage of human development and speciation. It affirms the mystery of being human in that each of us has a local purpose and a larger purpose—some might even say a global purpose. Taken together, these purposes call us toward greater awareness and higher usefulness. Please remember: You are not an encapsulated bag of skin dragging around a dreary little ego. You are instead a symbiosis of person, planet, self, nature, mind, and spirit. As you will discover in the course of experiencing this book, you are all these things plus much, much more. Ultimately, you are in partnership with Creation itself. Whether you call it God, or the Quantum Ground of Being, or the Mind of the Universe, or the Spirit that informs us all, it is that Beingness which holds all potentials, all possibilities, and with which we can cocreate. For, as we discover, not only do we live in the universe, but also the universe lives in us. And thus, all acts of creation and becoming are acts of *cocreation.*

Jean Houston, PhD
Author, scholar, philosopher, researcher in Human Capacities

Acknowledgments

For years I wrote articles and blogs only loosely connected by a general theme of inner change work. Bridget Reynolds, marketing manager, friend, and confidante, saw these unified into a single, powerful message to create much-needed change in consciousness. For her, the writings were like pattern pieces waiting to be sewn together to create something useful. It was her insightful vision that gave me the courage to write *Change Within, Change the World*. She held that vision when I could not see how the pieces could come together, guiding me to produce not another self-help book but a needed impetus to create necessary paradigm shifts. I am indebted to her for extensive and in-depth research, which made her akin to a coauthor. She would read what I had written and point out the places where more was needed, urgently prodding me to motivate my audience. She saw the need for externally understanding our condition before diving into internal processes. Her guiding brilliance shines through the book.

A moment arrives when a book comes alive, when it takes on a life of its own apart from author or reader. Pinocchio was a wooden puppet who longed to become a real boy, alive and growing, and like Pinocchio, this book came alive somewhere in the editing process with Hilary Tate. The satisfaction we felt after crafting a phrase or paragraph into a gourmet delight stretched our editing days into pure joy. The alchemy of a good editor like Hilary is magical!

Finally, thanks to Dr. Jean Houston, my mentor and friend, who taught me to think in the four levels: sensory, psychological, mythic, and unitive. Many years of being inspired by her, from her Mystery School and salon to her books and lectures, have guided, shaped, and yes, stretched my thinking processes, making this book possible.

Preface

The Night I Arm-Wrestled with Fear

When I was in my thirties, I heard about a woman who was beaten to death in full view of her neighbors, who were so afraid that not one came to her aid or even called the police. I promised myself that if I ever were confronted with a similar situation, I would not let fear hold me back from getting involved.

In those days, I was living in the Haight-Ashbury in San Francisco. About midnight one night, returning from the theater with my boss and her husband, I saw two burly young men on a street corner, shoving and punching each other. Without thinking, I walked over to them and said, "You stop that this minute! This is my street corner, and I don't want any fighting here!" Just then a car pulled up and six other men got out and started egging the fighters on. I told them to stop the fighting, that I didn't want any of that here on my street. When the six pulled the initial men apart, the verbal fight escalated, so I stepped between them. One of the men from the car yelled at me to get out of there or I would get hurt, that this was serious! I shouted back, "Well then, *you* get in here!" Without hesitation, he replied, "Not me, I'm gay!" With that non sequitur, that seemingly nonsensical reply, the steam went out of the confrontation and all of the men disappeared.

To this day, I don't know why those tough guys even listened to a tiny woman scolding them—at midnight in the Haight! And I don't know what made me do such a dangerous and foolish thing. But somehow I felt that I had proven my resolve and could trust myself to become involved where necessary.

For me, inner change is the key to changing the external world. Much of my life has been about change—changing what seems impossible, changing deeply embedded, limiting beliefs, and changing physical and mental conditions, both for me and for clients.

My journey is certainly not unique. Yet it has taken me many places and revealed talents that I would otherwise not have recognized. The studies that have attracted me over the years are the disciplines of energy work and inner change: Reiki, NeuroLinguistic Programming (NLP), hypnotherapy, and Huna, the esoteric art of Hawaiian spirituality and psychology, to name a few. After becoming an Essene minister, I increasingly incorporated the spiritual dimension into my work with clients. As I learned different body and massage techniques, my hands began to express a wisdom that my head had no idea about. This drew me to study the Hawaiian massage lomilomi on the Big Island with Auntie Margaret Machado, for whom massage with loving hands is "praying" work. As I deepened my skills, I was eager to share the new possibilities for change. It soon became apparent that my interests were so diverse that I was going to have to specialize in a few or find an umbrella under which I could lump them all. When the phrase "change within" came to me in a meditation, I realized that here was the umbrella for all my practices. I didn't have to choose one discipline over another. Once I figured that out, my practices took off.

But life has a way of not letting me rest on my laurels. My life changed radically at age forty, when I married for the first time: moving to Southern California from San Francisco, where I had a close network of friends; becoming an instant stepmother; buying a home; spending long, tedious hours commuting through LA traffic to a corporate managerial job supervising one hundred employees with budgets and union negotiations. Soon the stress of these multiple changes expressed itself as enervating, itchy blotches all over. For six years, uncomfortable in my own bloated body, I blamed my miserable state on an allergy to my bed. Finally, when my doctor asked me what I was refusing to look at in my marriage, I realized

I felt trapped. This awareness prompted me to begin the lengthy process of reclaiming my life.

During this time, in an NLP class, I volunteered to be a demonstration subject for the use of a pendulum. Through a series of yes–no questions, the instructor asked if and when my body would be willing to heal, and the pendulum signaled that the healing would begin in one month. And a month later, I woke up feeling as though a bad case of flu had left my body. For the first time in six years, I felt *good*. My long years of pain and stress had served as a shamanic death and rebirth experience, which awakened new intuitive skills. After that, I started combining the disciplines I had studied with the techniques I had invented.

The next area I explored was the eye-brain connection. My sister, Martha, and I wrote *Eye Yoga: How you see is how you think,* giving simple eye exercises that can awaken deep brain capacities. We started to write a 40-page booklet of eye exercises anyone can do with little or no equipment, and it grew to 340 pages of eye-brain connections and techniques to increase brain neuroplasticity. It has helped many, from improving eyesight to recovering from stroke debilitations. The techniques are detailed in my DVDs, *Brain Yoga: Increase Your Brain Power* and *Eye Yoga Tips.*[1]

Following the Muse[2] of Change, who seems to nudge me along a variety of paths, I intended to turn a series of blogs into a second book. This material has morphed into a fervent, persistent cry for the world as *Change Within, Change the World.*

CHANGE

is a door
that can only be
opened from the
INSIDE

Photograph by Ron Cordek

Introduction

Change Within, Change the World is divided into two parts. Like the phrase "as above, so below," the polarity and symmetry of "as within, so without" are expressed in the book's inextricable link between Part One—External Reality and Part Two—Internal Change. Our external reality and our internal landscape are entwined because our internal perceptions create our personal reality. To change the external, we have to change the internal. In this way the book is about change—change in the midst of chaos. It's also about hope.

A word in current usage among younger generations is *woke*, which is increasingly used as a byword for being self-aware, questioning the dominant paradigm, and striving for social and racial justice. A major premise of this book is that waking up—staying woke—entails a unique responsibility for each of us. Falling back into obsolete ways of being is dangerous, and our present institutions aren't going to save us. Many years ago, Mahatma Gandhi said that we have to be the change we wish to see in the world.[3] This means, in concrete terms, that each of us has to become a model of the change we long for. If we bring such vestiges of the old model as patriarchy, racism, and greed into the new, then we run the risk of putting a Band-Aid on our dying culture, when major surgery is needed.

Part One examines our external reality. The writings and theories of writers/scientists about the historic cycles of our evolution reveal how we have arrived at our current stage. From these writings, it's clear that this cycle is in its dying throes and needs to be transformed. Refusal or inability to bring about such transformation has the potential to take us to extinction. The situation is dire. But all over the world people are waking up to the knowledge that our structural foundation is disintegrating and its ability to hold things together has run its course. Dissent and movements abound.

Part Two deals with internal change. It is my core belief that we can only accomplish the external changes so necessary to our survival by changing within. The reason for dividing Part Two into sections is the answer to the question, How do you eat an elephant? The answer is, One bite at a time. Skill development is easier when it's divided into chunks. The skills are presented with fundamentals first, and then come more subtle techniques.

I have developed the processes through years of work with my clients and on myself. They are intended to guide deep and honest inquiry in order to identify those vestiges of the old model that we still embody, that we have to uproot and heal. We need to find the areas where we cling to fear, self-doubt, competition, judgment, and the like. We need to recognize how committed we are to replacing them with their opposites—courage, self-esteem, partnership, and acceptance.

The time when we could put off dealing with these matters is long past. They are the task of our time and our generations. On every global issue, we've passed the eleventh hour and reached the twelfth hour for dealing with economic disparities, poverty, world hunger, torture, climate change, cybercrime, wealth inequities, child abuse, gender inequality, terrorism, and mass forced migrations, to name a few. No longer can a single nation solve any of these issues alone, certainly not a single individual. I was highly motivated to do something, but I didn't know where to start. Realizing that, I grappled with despair over these crises; it was as frightening as trying to combat a forest fire with a fire extinguisher!

When I read Jean Houston's *Jump Time*, I was inspired to reconsider that realization. Jump Time, as she defines it, is a sudden shift of the "same old, same old" in a short period of time. It is

> the changing of the guard on every level, in which every "given" is quite literally up for grabs. It is the momentum behind the drama of the world, the breakdown and breakthrough of every old way of being,

knowing, relating, governing and believing. It shakes
the foundation of all and everything. And it allows for
another order of reality to come into being.[4]

As a cultural historian, Dr. Houston studies patterns of history. She
believes that in this time, when all our social structures are breaking
down, something exhilarating and unique may happen—or we may
not survive.

At a time when whole systems are in transition and
global forces challenge all authority, there is an insistence
in the mud, contractions shiver through the Earth womb,
patterns of possibility strain to emerge from the rough
clay of changing social structures.[5]

It is, she says, a matter of kairos, a potent time for fortuitous
happenings.

This is a clear call to action, and I've never let an emotion as
puny as fear keep me from what I'm drawn to do. In reflecting on
the steps I have taken to challenge fear, I discovered that I look for
areas where I can create new perspectives—beliefs, values, and views
of what is possible—to replace what no longer serves me. That is, I
find where I can change myself *within*. I become more informed.
From some innate understanding that I don't have to do it alone,
I look for like-minded people to partner with. My commitment to
my own emotional, psychological, and spiritual well-being has led
me to professions in which I work with others who have a similar
commitment.

I offer this book of techniques for change, some that I've
developed and all that I've used, as my contribution to a better world.
Those who have searched for ways to shift the present paradigm
and its consciousness may find value here. Younger generations
may uncover fresh ideas to support their own revolutionary notions.
Both those who have long striven for change and today's courageous
young people are frustrated by what passes for leadership. This book

presents skills for manifesting a lifesaving, world-saving agenda—by changing within and changing the world simultaneously.

May this book entice you to examine yourself—your values, beliefs, visions, and strengths. I hope it gives you tools for going deep and honing your inner skills. Changing within changes everything.

> Not everything that is faced can be changed but nothing can be changed until it is faced.[6]
>
> —James Baldwin

Part One
External Reality

We study a map to plot the course to our destination. But essential to getting there is knowing where we are before we set out. In studying history's large repeating patterns, or fractals, we learn not only where we are in the big picture but also how we got here and what may be in store for the future. When the immediate appears chaotic, the map of history's fractals can make our situation more comprehensible.

> If you don't know where you've come from it's very difficult to see what the possibilities are for where you're headed.[7]
>
> —Elisabet Sahtouris

To provide such a map, I have rummaged through an array of topics and authors, searching for themes and trends that might give us clarity, direction, and hope. In this review of our external reality, I first address how we got here. Then I look for where we may have power to affect our future, places that we may have overlooked.

Section I

How We Got Here:
Historical Review

Chapter 1

Consciousness Evolution: Jean Gebser

I started with Jean Gebser (1905–1975), Swiss philosopher, linguist, and poet, a man of extraordinary vision. He studied the structures of human consciousness and their transitions as they evolve. He identifies these five stages:

- Archaic structure of consciousness is instinctual, primal. With no subject–object differentiation, man is vaguely aware of himself in the world around him as he merges with nature.
- Magic structure is egocentric, a transition from the one-dimensional, undifferentiated state of Archaic. With rudimentary recognition of himself as an entity, man is impelled by the survival instinct.
- Mythical structure, traditional, becomes two-dimensional as man disengages from unity with nature and develops a sense of self and ego. Tool making and banding together into larger social structures with gods, religion, and shamanic endeavors become important. As mankind expands its imagination, the soul and the afterlife, as seen in the Egyptian culture, for example, become concerns.
- Mental/Rational structure is our current stage. This shift took place between 10,000 and 500 BCE. Mankind steps into a three-dimensional world where abstraction, philosophy, and perspective become possible. Language adds a spatial quality as individuation from nature takes

over. Man's rational mind refuses to accept anything without questioning and analysis.

- Integral structure is postmodern. It incorporates all the previous structures of consciousness, enabling the human mind to transcend the limits of three-dimensionality and enter a fourth-dimensional reality. With love as the energy driving spiritual growth of this consciousness, people operate as a whole, recognizing themselves in others. Cooperation and peaceful resolutions of issues characterize this stage.

Like all the stages, the Rational is a mixed blessing. On the one hand, we have developed a highly individual mind that refuses to adopt anything without questioning or analysis. We've gained perspective, moving from two dimensions to three in our view, as reflected, for example, in the shift from the flat, two-dimensional paintings of the Middle Ages to the Renaissance works with three-dimensional depth. On the other hand, this structure has created many tensions. We feel that there's never enough time, that time is money, and that we're killing time. We see ourselves as separate from nature. The motorizing, mechanizing, and technologizing of our lives has led to an immeasurable loss of freedom. The time sinkholes of video games and the internet lead to mediocrity and addiction. Sports, once a form of play and of honing war skills, have become a frenzy of record-keeping and record-setting. Athletes are more interested in monetary rewards than the love of the game—top football players, for instance, frequently open themselves to the NFL draft while still freshmen in college. Our current materialistic trend is perhaps the final stage of the Rational/Mental structure. Fortunately, according to Gebser, the tensions of the transitional era we are in will catapult us into our next significant leap of consciousness, from the Rational to the Integral Structure.

The Integral Structure makes use of and transcends all the previous structures, seeing the entirety rather than the competing parts. Since the world is viewed as a connected whole, issues are settled peacefully by taking into consideration the needs of the other structures in relationship to the whole. Hallmarks of this emerging stage include integrity, transparency, spirituality, renunciation of power and dominance, connection to the whole, and replacement of patriarchy with nonhierarchical systems.

Gebser's vision depicted a global situation that has only magnified and intensified in its complexity and unmanageable hugeness. Gebser saw humans in a final stage of consciousness development, a make-or-break point, as we transition to the Integral Structure of consciousness. His point that something must give way or evolve means that a shift in consciousness is essential. He described it thus:

> At present mankind is undergoing an evolutionary crisis in which is concealed a choice of its destiny; for a stage has been reached in which the human mind has achieved in certain directions an enormous development while in others it stands arrested and bewildered and can no longer find its way. ... Man has created a system of civilisation which has become too big for his limited mental capacity and understanding and his still more limited spiritual and moral capacity to utilise and manage, a too dangerous servant of his blundering ego and its appetites.[8]

Gebser sees that if we are to evolve to the Integral stage, it is essential that we acquire the mental and spiritual skills we lack in our current Rational/Mental stage.

Chapter 2

Complexification and the Noosphere: Pierre Teilhard de Chardin, Rupert Sheldrake, Jose Arguelles

I next looked to Pierre Teilhard de Chardin (1881–1955), philosopher, paleontologist, and Jesuit priest, who famously said, "We are not human beings having a spiritual experience. We are spiritual beings having a human experience."[9]

He saw humans continuing to complexify until we arrive at a terminal position, which he called the Omega Point. The Omega Point is where we

- organically can't go any further in complexity, and therefore our consciousness is also limited;
- psychically can't accept the failure of falling back to an earlier state; yet
- human yearning is such that cosmically we cannot remain in one place—we must continually strive to move forward.

According to Teilhard, we must shift our most fundamental assumptions or perish. It's like the caterpillar in its cocoon that must turn to mush and then transform into a butterfly or die. Our survival requires a quantum leap in consciousness.

Teilhard believed that a global network of human beings would evolve to an entity of even higher complexity and consciousness. He said, "Our duty, as men and women, is to proceed as if limits to our ability did not exist. We are collaborators in creation."[10] Not limiting this concept to humans or even to the external world, he explained as follows:

> The time has come to realize that an interpretation of the universe—even a positivist one—remains unsatisfying unless it covers the interior as well as the exterior of things; mind as well as matter. The true physics is that which will, one day, achieve the inclusion of man in his wholeness in a coherent picture of the world.[11]

The other concept that Teilhard thought vitally important was the noosphere. He suggested that in its evolutionary unfolding, the earth was growing a new organ of consciousness. As the earth's body is the biosphere, its mind is the noosphere. He regarded it literally as the earth's mental sheath, a highly charged thinking layer that acts as a mind field of collective consciousness. It is there to join us together into a level of unity previously unknown. Our yearning for the whole and for oneness is what compels us to the Omega Point. Yet it is much more, transcending our humanity and linking us to a quantum-reality metaverse of a collective virtual shared space. Again, I refer to his own words so as not to lose the beauty and essence:

> There is almost a sensual longing for communion with others who have a large vision. The immense fulfillment of the friendship between those engaged in furthering the evolution of consciousness has a quality impossible to describe.[12]

> Remain true to yourself, but move ever upward toward greater consciousness and greater love! At the summit you will find yourselves united with all those who, from every direction, have made the same ascent. For everything that rises must converge.[13]

> The age of nations has passed. Now, unless we wish to perish, we must shake off our old prejudices and build the Earth. The more scientifically I regard the world,

the less I can see any biological future for it except in the active consciousness of its unity.[14]

The idea of a common field for the earth's collective consciousness is not new. Carl Jung equated it to synchronicity and a telepathic medium of communication. The theory of the noosphere was intrinsic to Buckminster Fuller's concepts for a whole-system design of the earth as an evolving organism.[15] It's the earth's internet! One of my favorite examples of this is known as the "Hundredth Monkey Effect." Rupert Sheldrake, a Cambridge-trained biochemist, physiologist, and prominent public intellectual, proposes that every species has a morphic field of thought to which all its members contribute. When one hundred monkeys on one island began washing their sweet potatoes to get the sand off, monkeys on other islands, who had never seen this activity, spontaneously began to do the same. In short order, monkeys all over the world picked it up. What one hundred monkeys started became accessible to all monkeys through this monkey morphic field. Whether legend or fact, this story illustrates the phenomenon of critical mass and morphic field. It is true that when mice in England learned to run mazes faster, mice in the United States also began learning faster, even though the two groups of mice did not have the benefit of physical contact with each other. And what about humans? Roger Bannister was the first to run a mile in under four minutes. In less than a month, John Landy beat Bannister's record. In 2015 a high school student, Matthew Maton, was the sixth high schooler to break four minutes! We seem to be able to stand on the shoulders of those before us. Sheldrake calls this long-distance learning "nonlocal resonance" and says that it allows habits to be shared across space without physical contact.

According to Sheldrake, *morphogenetic* means "giving birth to form." His theory of formative causation is concerned with how things, from galaxies to atoms, take up their forms or patterns and organize themselves. He calls the self-organizing systems their fields. The forms of each system depend on the way the previous ones of that kind were organized. According to his theory, there is a built-in memory of each kind of thing.

The fields are generally defined as regions of influence. When asked what these fields are made of, his answer is that nobody really knows. Called morphic fields, they are structures in space and time, localized in and around the system they organize. So the morphic field of us as humans is in and around us, resonating and influencing other human fields in morphic resonance. He suggests the probability of invisible mathematical laws at work, which, although not material or energetic, are nevertheless mysteriously always present everywhere.

Sheldrake's hypothesis upsets mechanistic science while demonstrating its limitations. It gives a completely new view of instincts and behavioral patterns and also provides a new understanding of social structures and cultural ideas. Each pattern organized by a field—a social group, for example—has an inherent, collective memory upon which we all draw. It not only organizes the present but also contains a memory of that particular group in the past and, through morphic resonance, a memory of previously existing similar social groups.

> The universe is not in a steady state; there's an ongoing creative principle in nature, which is driving things onwards.[16]
>
> —Rupert Sheldrake

The cumulative nature of the evolutionary process, the idea that memory is preserved, means not just that life grows through a random proliferation of new forms but also that there is a kind of cumulative quality to it all.

The most compelling implication in his hypothesis is that nature is not governed by externally fixed laws but rather by habits that are able to evolve as conditions change. He feels that the natural world in which we live, and indeed the entire cosmos, is alive. It is a vast, constantly evolving organism with developing habits. This is contrary to the mechanistic idea that nature is a fixed machine governed by fixed laws. His work provides insights into how new patterns of activity can spread far more quickly than would have been thought possible under standard mechanistic theories, asserting that if many people start doing, thinking, or practicing something, it will make it easier for others to do the same.

Here's an example of nonlocal resonance, in this case, the swift spreading of an idea worldwide. The ancient Maya used a long-count calendar in which 13 b'ak'tuns, or 5,125 years, came to an end on December 21, 2012. Jose Arguelles unraveled the Mayan calendar matrix and found two significant dates. The first, August 1987, came to be known as the Harmonic Convergence. It was a key time for us to access the noosphere for planetary peace.[17] In August 1987, millions of people worldwide joined in a globally synchronized, nonlocal meditation and prayer at key sacred sites to seed a world vision for a peaceful future. Shortly after, strange, unpredicted events occurred, such as the fall of the Berlin Wall and the unraveling of the Soviet Union. Could the morphic resonance of humans have been affected by the global synchronized thought of the Harmonic Convergence?

The second date of importance was the culmination of the Mayan calendar on December 21, 2012, and there were many interpretations of what was going to happen, including the end of the world. Since the world did not end, I like the interpretation of Ricardo Cajas, president of the Colectivo de Organizaciones Indigenas de Guatemala, who said the date didn't represent an end of humanity but initiated a new calendar involving changes in human consciousness.[18] Arguelles posited that after the end of the thirteen b'ak'tuns, humans might become a totally different species. Ever since, I have been watching to see what would happen. If we can collectively shift the world by inner meditation and change work, if we can contribute to the noosphere or the human morphic field, there is hope, there are possibilities for action. Joining with others in this collective thought field could make a difference.

Chapter 3

Values Levels: Clare Graves, Don Beck and Chris Cowan, Ken Wilber, Frederic Laloux, Said Dawlabani

Dr. Clare Graves (1914–1986) initiated values levels work. Maintaining that humans evolve in an increasingly complex way in their cultures and corresponding values, he mapped the levels of human existence and their evolving bio-psychosocial values structures. To give yourself a general picture of these levels, in your imagination, first invent a culture that draws on magical rites to appease nature and the gods. Then see this society evolving to one of warring chieftains, each defending his turf. It may progress to an orderly polity ruled by a king, where everyone knows their place and job. Then an entrepreneurial, individualistic system evolves, with competition for money and resources. People rebel against this "me first" capitalism and join groups such as Greenpeace to defend the earth.

Dr. Graves writes about these levels as a never-ending quest:

> At each stage of human existence the adult man is off on his quest for his holy grail, the way of life he seeks by which to live. At his first level he is on a quest for automatic physiological satisfaction. At the second level he seeks a safe mode of living, and this is followed in turn by a search for heroic status, for power and glory; by a search for ultimate peace; a search for material pleasure, a search for affectionate relations, a search for respect of

self, and a search for peace in an incomprehensible world. And, when he finds he will not find that peace, he will be off on his ninth level quest. As he sets off on each quest, he believes he will find the answer to his existence. Yet, much to his surprise and dismay, he finds at every stage the solution to existence is not the solution he has come to find. Every state he reaches leaves him disconcerted and perplexed. It is simply that as he solves one set of human problems he finds a new set in their place. The quest he finds is never ending.[19]

A number of theorists have been influenced by Dr. Graves's Emergent Cyclical Levels of Existence Theory. Don Beck and Chris Cowan used it as the basis for their book *Spiral Dynamics: Mastering Values, Leadership, and Change.* Integral theorist, philosopher, and creative spiritual thinker Ken Wilber referenced the values levels extensively in *A Theory of Everything* and subsequent work. Frederic Laloux applied the values levels to creating organizations inspired by a higher form of consciousness. His book *Reinventing Organizations* describes how large and small organizations can operate in this new paradigm. And finally, cultural economist and theorist Said Dawlabani applied it to economics, where he used it to predict the market crash of 2008. These explorations of the ramifications of values levels mirror Gebser's work with levels of consciousness, which took place around the time of World War I and Einstein's development of the theory of relativity.

The authors mentioned above generally agree that there are currently eight values levels in human existence with distinct characteristics for each, such as social and economic behaviors, priorities, and ways of thinking. Each level represents a phase of development for individuals within a group and for subgroups operating within the larger culture. Each also exists as a structure in the brain. You can use these levels to help understand yourself, other people, social groups, and societies. If you can identify the level at which people are existing, then you can find the language to communicate with them and the values to which they will respond.

The values are grouped in tiers or batches of six. The jump from the values in Tier 1 to the values in Tier 2 represents a paradigm shift, a radical leap in thinking, perspective, and worldview.

Using color codings for ease of identification, here is a brief description of the six values of Tier 1:

Color	Values	Expressions
Beige	Survival	Food, water, shelter, procreation
Purple	Tribes, kin spirits	Rites, taboos, superstitions
Red	Warlords, chieftains	Gangs, mafia, authoritarianism, conquests
Blue	Institutions, truth, law, and order	Tradition, rules, morality, patriotism, obedience to authority, conformity, Catholic Church, national government
Orange	Entrepreneur, competition	Personal success, money over loyalty, strive/drive, capitalism
Green	Consensus, environment	Group bonding, community, being liked over competitive advantage, Greenpeace

These values spiral up in complexity and sophistication as they evolve back and forth between an individualistic, expressive mode (red, orange) and a communal, sacrificial one (blue, green). Each stage in Tier 1 thinks it alone is right and the others are wrong.

Then something different happens when the values shift to Tier 2. This is the first time that "both–and" and "win–win" thinking come into being. People achieve the capacity to hold multiple perspectives simultaneously. Here the worldview is large enough to include all the partial truths and values of previous stages. Even though cultures can remain at their present level, today's constant conflict is replaced with all-embracing world culture and deep harmony. Tier 2 will remake human nature and culture as we know it. Let's take a look at what these radically different values might look like.

Tier 2 starts with yellow, Flex Flow, where natural systems, multiple realities, and learning for its own sake are important. At this level, these qualities and values assume greater importance:

- dealing with uncertainty, complexity, and integration of complex systems
- ideas, systems thinking, and the interaction of parts to create a greater whole
- respect for the problem-solving abilities of knowledge and information rather than status and materialism
- deep understanding of ecology in a more subdued, behind-the-scenes way
- appreciation of functionality
- recognizing the unique abilities and idiosyncrasies of each level in order to behave appropriately and contextually

Yellows, on the one hand, value diversity and respect other cultures. They look at the big picture and long-term consequences. They often work on the periphery, quietly fine-tuning situations and procedures. On the other hand, they tend to withdraw from group activities and become individualistic. They tend not to vote, don't go to therapy, don't join groups or clubs, and prefer to work alone and in small groups of like-minded people. They feel misunderstood and think it's lonely at the top.

The next level, Whole View, known as turquoise or teal, is holistic. It is the best we as a species have attained so far. Collective individualism, cosmic spirituality, and earth changes are important. Work must be meaningful to the overall health of life. Feelings and information join to enhance experience. Teal consciousness honors many perspectives structured in multidimensional ways. It is aware of energy fields and holographic links. It uses collective human intelligence to work on large-scale problems without sacrificing individuality. Spiritual connection combines with technology to protect the earth. It takes a tough love approach to threats to survival of the planet and its inhabitants. It recognizes the need to work with global consciousness as well as the more local realms of home, community, and nation as it transcends group identity. For example, teal people function *in* groups but not *as* groups. They are obsessed with including exploration of consciousness and its simultaneous levels in their endeavors. They identify with the concept of "as above, so below" and repeating patterns of the microcosm in the macrocosm.

Like new shoots of daffodils poking up from the cold earth in early spring, examples of organizations adopting this new values level thinking are sprouting up. They are well described in Frederic Laloux's book *Reinventing Organizations* (2014). Teal organizations work in matrices of small decentralized teams rather than in a pyramid, top-down hierarchy. The organization is viewed as having an evolutionary purpose, a life and sense of direction of its own. It is this purpose, rather than a president or CEO driving the corporation to make profits, that directs their work. Individuals ask for suggestions but ultimately make their own decisions and have autonomy to do so as long as they keep the group informed. If they need resources, they present their case to the whole. If one person isn't doing their job, it is the responsibility of another team member to work with them to determine what resources they need to get the job done. Sometimes an individual decides the job isn't for them and quits, but there is little firing. Laloux studied twelve companies with a teal approach. The wide array of teal companies includes Patagonia (apparel), Sounds True (media), Sun Hydraulics (hydraulic components), Buurtzorg (Netherlands; health care), FAVI (French; metal manufacturing), and Morning Star (United States; food processing).

For three years I have had the experience of watching a group of emerging young adult leaders of Social Artistry (a series of processes whereby individuals activate their potential and acquire skills for creating positive changes in the world), along with their elder mentors, use the teal approach in planning and executing their annual Odyssey training program for over one hundred attendees. Under this radically different approach, young adults have transformed into skillful communicators, responsible organizers, and heart-centered motivators. Thanks to the training and mentoring she received, a young mother of three from a public housing project in Georgia has traveled to twenty-three countries, teaching techniques for engaging people in community projects, all the while homeschooling her children. A shy young man with no job is now employed and travels all over his home state to colleges and schools to recruit other young adults to the Social Artistry Odyssey. These and many other examples give me hope for this new approach.

> You never change things by fighting the existing reality.
> To change something, build a new model that makes the existing model obsolete.[20]
>
> —Buckminster Fuller

Various sources, including Ken Wilber and Don Beck, put the percentage of the world's individuals at Tier 2 levels between 5 percent and 8 percent, saying that when 10 percent operate at these levels, we will have reached a tipping point, and the rest will be pulled toward this new evolution in consciousness.

Given recent events, it's possible that we have now passed the necessary 10 percent. The first truly inclusive, nonoppressive culture in humankind's entire history could begin to emerge, and we could be cocreators. It is coming just in time, since most of humankind's problems are now global. Actions by individual nations have become useless. If, for example, one nation were to cut its carbon emissions to zero, it would have little effect on the whole. For a solution to work, all nations must participate.

Systemic planetary problems such as global warming, overpopulation, and terrorism demand integral solutions, not piecemeal ones. Partial, fragmented solutions hurt rather than help. The sooner individuals adopt integrative thinking, the better chance we have.

Chapter 4

Biological Evolution: Elisabet Sahtouris

From the writings of acclaimed evolutionary biologist, futurist, and author Elisabet Sahtouris, I learned that science rests on cultural assumptions and beliefs about the nature of the universe. Is it a nonliving universe in which matter evolves accidentally, eventually producing human consciousness? Is it a vast machine to be studied objectively? Or, on the other hand, is it a living universe in which consciousness precedes and gives rise to matter? Is it a participatory universe in which we affect what we are observing?

Dr. Sahtouris realized that the basic assumptions of Western science's Darwinian, mechanistic approach are limiting. The Darwinian view posits a dead universe in which accidental mutations cause evolution and only the fittest survive. Nature is not intelligent. Life is a struggle for scarce resources. With not enough to go around, only the strong survive. Fierce competition is human nature's creation story. This worldview has given us an economy driven by consumption that is liquidating the planet's assets. We are in the sixth global extinction biologically, the first one to be caused by one species.

Realizing that the parameters on which science is built determine its findings, Sahtouris rejected the premise and the implications of Western science. Instead she adopted a radically different approach, a Vedic science based on a living universe. The fundamental Vedic assumption is that everything starts from living, intelligent, interactive cosmic consciousness, and within that unity the individuation of matter arises. We have forgotten that we are part of the whole, Sahtouris says, and see ourselves as disconnected individuals. Nature is alive, intelligent, and conscious down to its subatomic particles. It is self-organizing and participatory. Nature conserves the things that work well and is radically creative when things do not work. We are in the universe, and everything we do, including observation, affects what we are observing.

In searching for what nature can teach us that will help us create a better future, Sahtouris began with the evolution of bacteria, the earliest life on our planet. For two billion years (half its life), the earth was populated only by bacteria, whose rampant reproduction caused worldwide crises of hunger and pollution. At this juvenile stage, the bacteria's behavior was Darwinian and highly competitive; they scarfed up resources, hogged territory, multiplied wildly, and were eventually threatened with extinction. But nature seems to understand that crises drive evolution. This feisty pioneering stage of competing for resources is only one side of nature's process. Cooperation is the other side, and when bacterial life was threatened with extinction, it evolved toward a mature, cooperative stage. An ecosystem with negotiated rather than violent outcomes appeared. Conflicts were resolved, and in the best-case scenarios not only did real cooperation develop but also a new unity at a more complex level arose. This is where the big steps in evolution took place. The bacteria harnessed solar energy, created oxygen, and then invented breathing and an electric motor that used the oxygen productively. They created the first worldwide web of DNA information trade. They evolved the huge, cooperative, nucleated cell, which became the new species on the planet, leading to a competitive youth of another billion years. Eventually those cells arrived at the place in the maturation cycle where they formed larger cooperatives, multicellular creatures. All that was done by bacteria without benefit of a brain. Clearly intelligence was at work.

As humans we have evolved from bacteria, and we follow the same evolutionary cycles of competition and cooperation. We have survived a dozen ice ages in cooperative communities that included other species. But six thousand years of expansion, conquering, and empire building have put us back in the immature competition mode. The present situation can be frightening, but crisis impels us to become cooperative. The biggest crises have produced the most wonderful cooperatives. Globalization is creating the predicament in which we must make the transition to a cooperative stage, in which we can create a sustainable global economy and become a global family. If we fail, we will bring about our extinction.

> Every time humanity has shifted to a new stage, it has invented a new way to collaborate, a new organizational model.[21]
>
> —Frederic Laloux

Sahtouris says that change comes suddenly, in distinct quantum leaps. She has noticed that young people of today (Millennials and those younger) are showing little interest in racism or hate or greed. Feelings are becoming important, as evidenced by such simple things as the explosion in popularity of emojis. On the internet, young people are resonating with each other and building bridges across minds. In the previous discussion of the Maya calendar, the idea was posed that at the end of the thirteen-b'ak'tun cycle, humankind could literally become a new species. Recently there has been an increase in transparency and telepathy. First, we had revelations coming out in the corporate world (Enron's unethical practices) and then in the church (sex abuse scandals), and now in government (Snowden and other whistleblowers leaking NSA's global surveillance programs). Many young people are exploring telepathy as another form of transparency, a human birthright, resonant with many indigenous cultures. Sahtouris, for example, observes that young people today, through social media communication, are building a simplified shorthand of abbreviations and emoticons:

> By reducing the amount of text and adding symbols for emotions something very interesting is going on because the person you're talking to knows how you're feeling in that moment and that sets up an energy field. This can

communicate without time-space interference. When you don't have to think up so many words and are making this emotional connection, you are setting up a situation in which telepathy can build very easily.[22]

Perhaps our new species will emerge as soon as the next few generations. Imagine a nonideological, peaceful revolution toward a better life coming so soon.

We are learning that there is more than one way to organize functional systems, to produce order and balance; that the imperfect and flexible principles of nature lead to greater stability and resilience in natural systems than we have produced in ours—both technological and social—by following the mechanical laws we assumed were natural. ... On the whole, there seems to be good reason to believe our species' recklessly egotistical and destructive phase is coming to an end with new knowledge that leads us back to ancient wisdom. We are capable of regaining our reverence for life, of replacing the drive to conquer with the will to cooperate, of remaking our engineered institutions, including our corporations, into living systems.[23]

Chapter 5

Global Risks and Interconnections: World Economic Forum

The information for this section comes mainly from the 2016, 2017, and 2018 Global Risk Reports by the World Economic Forum. They are based on the annual environmental report completed by 750 members of the forum's global multistakeholder community and on expert contributions from Zurich Insurance Group (a company operating on the teal values level) and other leading financial and academic institutions. In assessing global risks, the reports take into account degrees of impact and likelihood as well as interconnections in economic, environmental, geopolitical, societal, and technological areas. These factors are hugely interdependent, and a crisis in one area can quickly lead to crises in other areas, causing the breakdown of an entire system, as opposed to breakdowns in individual components. Modest tipping points can combine to produce large failures. In risk contagion,[24] a single loss can trigger a chain of other losses, leading to the loss of equilibrium in an entire system. Climate change, for example, is systemic, affecting all other areas. Water affects diseases, displacement of populations, and economies. Economic disparities are linked to global governance failures. The global risks reported in 2016, 2017, and 2018 are increasingly interconnected and elevated, making immediate actions more urgent now than ever.

The Global Risk Reports of the last three years show the following risks at the top of likelihood:

2016	2017	2018
Large-scale involuntary migration	Extreme weather	Extreme weather
Extreme weather	Large-scale involuntary migration	Natural disasters
Climate change mitigation failure	Natural disasters	Cyberattacks
Interstate conflicts	Large terrorist attack	Massive data fraud and theft
Natural catastrophic disasters	Massive data fraud and theft	Climate change mitigation failure

The risks at the top of impact for these three years are as follows:

2016	2017	2018
Climate change mitigation failure	Weapons of mass destruction	Weapons of mass destruction
Weapons of mass destruction	Extreme weather	Extreme weather
Water crises	Water crises	Major natural disasters
Large-scale involuntary migration	Major natural disasters	Climate change mitigation failure
Severe energy price shock	Climate change mitigation failure	Water crises

The risks at the top of the scale of both highest impact and likelihood for 2018 are weather and climate-related catastrophes, cyberattacks, and weapons of mass destruction, with this last at the very top of the impact scale.

In 2017, when these risks were mapped for their interconnections and resulting trends, climate change ranked alongside income inequality and societal polarization as top trends, with all five environmental risks appearing for the first time among the most likely and most impactful risks before the world. This continued into 2018 with high-impact hurricanes, record-breaking temperatures, and a rise in CO_2 emissions pushing our planet to the brink. For

2018 the highest interdependent risk was profound social instability, followed closely by extreme weather, involuntary migrations, unemployment and underemployment, and failures of national and regional governance. The following trends emerged from this panorama:

- rising cyberdependence
- changing climate
- increasing polarization of societies
- rising income and wealth disparity
- aging population

Other trends included the following:

- increasing national sentiment
- changing landscape of international governance
- shifting power
- rising urbanization
- degrading environment

The report makes some essential points. Global risks are increasingly complex and systemic. Because risks are interconnected, they cause a multiplier effect, requiring a holistic approach to risk management. A higher level of systems thinking and new ways of interdependent global collaboration are urgently needed. Multistakeholder involvements are a key strategy to building a better world. Even while globally we are enjoying the highest standards of living in human history, we are pushing the absorptive capacities of institutions, societies, and individuals to the limit, putting the future of human development at risk. This may be the first generation to bring the world to the edge of a systems breakdown.

Some observations from the 2018 Global Risk Report highlight these concerns:

> Humanity has become remarkably adept at understanding how to mitigate conventional risks that

can be relatively easily isolated and managed with standard risk management approaches. But we are much less competent when it comes to dealing with complex risks in the interconnected systems that underpin the world, such as organizations, economies, societies and the environment. There are signs of strain in many of these systems. ... When risk cascades through a complex system, the danger is not of incremental damage but of runaway collapse or an abrupt transition to a new, suboptimal status quo. [25]

As the pace of change accelerates, signs of strain are evident in many of the systems on which we rely. We cannot discount the possibility that one or more of these systems will collapse. Just as a piece of elastic can lose its capacity to snap back to its original shape, repeated stress can lead systems—organizations, economies, societies, the environment—to lose their capacity to rebound. If we exhaust our capacities to absorb the disruption and allow our systems to become brittle enough to break, it is difficult to overstate the damage that might result. [26]

It is heartening to recognize that groups and corporations are beginning to advocate global collaborative responses to these high risks, which have the markings of Gebser's integral structure, Teilhard's Omega Point, the values levels shift to Tier 2, and Sahtouris's shift to the mature cooperative stage in evolution biology. Some examples of entities making the shift and their impact are described in the following section. Similar themes are beginning to emerge. A number of retailers have entered into "green alliances" with environmental organizations to find ways to minimize their ecological footprints; they include Loblaw and Pollution Probe, S. C. Johnson and World Wildlife Fund, and McDonald's and the Environmental Defense Fund. Some of the companies whose environmental focus is saving water are the multinational beer giant SABMiller, multinational hospitality company Whitbread, and the United Kingdom's leading supermarket chain, Sainsbury's. The US companies Ben and Jerry's and Newman's Own have been modeling progressive practices for nearly forty years.

What is not so heartening is the admonition that our ability to absorb these risks is close to capacity. With conditions appearing so dire, it is encouraging to read the words of Dr. Paul Hawken:

> What I see everywhere in the world are ordinary people willing to confront despair, power, and incalculable odds in order to restore some semblance of grace, justice, and beauty to this world.[27]

Section II

What Gives Hope–Possible Ways to Affect Our World

In my research,[28] I set out to learn as much as possible about the big picture of where we are historically, to discover larger fractal patterns that would make current events more comprehensible when seen in a bigger picture. From that I hoped to uncover clues to a more intelligent path forward.

It's clear that we are at a crossroads, a make-or-break point for humanity, which is coming very quickly, and I still have the question of what to do about it that I had at the start of this book. Just waiting to see what will happen is not appealing to me. What have I found that gives me direction and hope? In a time when many feel powerless, where do we have power that we may have overlooked, discounted, or not recognized? And how can we use this power? I have come up with five sources that are making a positive impact for humanity. I invite you, the reader, to do your own thinking and research on this to come up with more places where we have power.

Chapter 6

NGOs

One of the first places where we have power that we have perhaps overlooked is in nongovernmental organizations (NGOs). A new phenomenon in the world, these are not-for-profit groups and institutions whose objectives are humanitarian or cooperative rather than commercial or political. They have power because they are not elected or profit-driven. Some are linked, but by and large they operate independently of each other, from local to international level, for humanitarian purposes. Like starfish, they have no head to chop off; when you cut off a leg, the starfish just grows another one. Individual NGOs wink in and out of existence all the time, yet NGOs continue to exist. They are dispersed and powerful, the biggest movement in history, a force of individuals for benevolence that cannot be eradicated.

Individuals often feel powerless when faced with political self-interests and governmental regulatory/financial power on the one hand and the wealth and self-serving greed of corporations on the other. What can balance these two forces? Picture the stability of a three-legged stool. NGOs function as a check-and-balance third power to political and corporate powers, much as the three branches of the US government, the judiciary, the executive, and the legislative branches, keep each other in check.

Today the estimated total number of NGOs ranges from 3.7 million to 10 million. If they were a country, they would represent the fifth-largest economy in the world! Their benevolent purposes include relief, providing information, lobbying, setting agendas, and generating norms to raise public awareness and influence governmental policy. Some mobilize disaster-relief resources to provide goods and services to people in need. Others act as catalysts to drive change by inspiring and contributing to improved thinking about human issues and problems. Some provide humanitarian intervention, while others present an independent voice. They have promoted environmental agreements, strengthened women's rights, and improved the well-being of children, the disabled, and the indigenous. Their levels of operation range from local and community to national and international. Their funding comes from memberships and donations ranging from individuals to corporations to governmental sources. Although they are not unified, nor could they be, they represent a very powerful collective.

In the political arena, the emphasis is usually on free elections and policy in accord with the wishes of the majority. However, in between elections the system must be transparent with a free flow of information about policy making. NGOs, while not affiliated with political parties or governmental agencies, contribute to global democracy by enhancing the flow of information within global governance. They report domestic politics to an international audience and bring global concerns and perspectives to national and local levels. They give voice to a broad constituency so that issues are considered within a wider perspective and different citizenries are heard. They are central to rising global political processes as we transition from international regimes and intergovernmental relations to global governance. They play a vital role in global decision-making with cross-border issues and multiple communities of interest, given that individual national governments cannot always do so as effectively or as legitimately.

Unlike the nonprofit NGOs, which are committed to the respective causes they represent, corporations are driven by their obligation to their stockholders and the bottom-line need for growth and profit. Because many are international in scope, they can be exempt from the will of the people of a nation. Their drive for profit over people is often mitigated by the work of NGOs to make them more socially responsible. The safety of products, the health risks associated with food and medicine, and the biological dangers of certain ingredients are a few areas where consumer-protection NGOs have demanded higher standards.

A few examples of some of the results and achievements of NGOs will give an overview of the vast influence and power of their collective power. The main purpose of Save the Children, one of the largest and oldest NGOs, is to improve socioeconomic conditions in developing countries. This organization has development-related projects in more than 120 countries, delivering services like health care and education and providing microcredit for communities. Amnesty International is an advocacy NGO, dedicated to promoting and defending human rights worldwide. The Widernet project, a small local NGO located in Iowa, provides a digital library to developing countries, especially in Africa. It strives to eradicate the digital gap between developed and developing countries. The NGO coalition International Campaign to Ban Land Mines was the prime mover in the Mine Ban Treaty of 1997. The Coalition for an International Criminal Court was indispensable to the adoption of the 1998 Treaty of Rome. In 1998, an NGO mobilization forced governments to abandon secret negotiations for the Multilateral Agreement on Investment. At the same time, an increasingly influential international NGO campaign demanded more just economic policies from the World Trade Organization, the International Monetary Fund, and the World Bank. Victories are often the result of the effective use of the internet, enabling rapid mobilization of global constituencies.

The January 2010 earthquake in Haiti gives an example of the ability of NGOs to respond expeditiously to emergencies. While the governments of Haiti and other nations were limited in their reactions, NGOs such as Oxfam International, the International Red Cross, World Vision, UNICEF, and the YMCA were among the first to offer aid. Other recognizable NGOs include CARE, Friends of the Earth, and Greenpeace.

Collectively, NGOs comprise the largest group of people working for a better society. They represent an alternative to the often self-serving interests of government and corporations, particularly those operating at the international level. They are the imaginal cells in the caterpillar cocoon that transform the mush into a butterfly. In the coming years, as the Tier 2 values of collaboration, altruism, and diversity reach a wider portion of the population, the need will grow for alternative visions and infrastructures that allow citizens to participate in the management of the global system. NGOs and their networks will be some of the most important early actors in an accountable, global, nongovernmental society.

Chapter 7

Cooperatives

Cooperatives are another alternative to corporate and political powers. The website of the National Co+op Grocers in the United States is called "Stronger Together," and that phrase sums up the power of cooperatives—individuals can accomplish more working together than working alone.

The International Cooperative Alliance defines a cooperative (a.k.a. co-op or coop) as "an autonomous association of persons united voluntarily to meet their common economic, social and cultural needs and aspirations through a jointly owned and democratically controlled enterprise."[29]

The range of co-op varieties worldwide is staggering: dairies in India; credit and savings societies in Kenya; electricity providers in France; a chain of banks in Switzerland; presses, renewable energy, and phone services in Britain; public transportation in Israel; insurance, home improvement supplies, and outdoor equipment in Canada; and medical care societies in New Zealand, to name a very few.[30] Environmentally and socially conscious Coop Kobe in Japan, with 1.2 million members, is the largest retail cooperative in the world.[31] Recognizable names in the United States include Ace Hardware, Associated Press, Blue Diamond almonds, Bob's Red Mill grain products, Diamond Walnuts, Land o' Lakes dairies, Ocean Spray cranberries, REI sporting goods and outdoor gear, Sunkist citrus, True Value Hardware, and Welch's—all co-ops.[32]

To succeed, co-ops must operate the way regular businesses do, with budgets, for example, accounting and management structure, but behind the scenes they are significantly different. Seven principles guide their transactions:

1. voluntary and open membership
2. democratic member control
3. member economic participation
4. autonomy and independence
5. education, training, and information
6. cooperation among cooperatives
7. concern for community.[33]

These principles produce such benefits as local rather than government or corporate control; greater buying power; lower costs; profit-sharing and refunds for members; and health, educational, humanitarian, and empowerment benefits for the community. They put decision-making and profit-sharing back into the hands of the members without leaching away huge sums of money for exorbitant bonuses, golden parachutes, bailouts, and payouts.

Like NGOs, co-ops are a substantial presence in world finance. In 2012, about one billion people in ninety-six countries were members of at least one co-op. The annual turnover reached $2.2 trillion. If co-ops were a country, they would be the world's seventh-largest economy.[34]

Chapter 8

The Noosphere and the Morphic Field

Our third source of power is the field of human thought, which is nested within the noosphere, that is, the earth's mental field. We can join forces to affect the human morphic field, a nonphysical field of information that instructs and shapes our evolution. It has a built-in memory sustained by morphic resonance. Whether this is via meditation and prayer synchronized globally or via like minds coming together locally, there is power in activating our mental fields. It took only one hundred monkeys to eventually change the habits of monkeys worldwide. Remember the powerful effects of the Harmonic Convergence, after which unexplainable events, such as the fall of the Berlin Wall, occurred, and remember our power through the internet to share thoughts, emotions, and ideas, with the World Wide Web acting as the earth's brain.

> The creative act is to let down the net of human imagination into the ocean of chaos on which we are suspended and then to attempt to bring out of it ideas.[35]
> —Rupert Sheldrake

To the extent that we can stay out of fear and magnify love, we make a positive contribution to the noosphere. Fear is an emotion that can protect us at times, but it is addicting and disempowering. Personally, I find that I must have a firm grip on my will to drop my habitual fears and focus on positive communal partnering.

> Fear is the cheapest room in the house.
> I would like to see you living
> In better conditions.[36]
>
> — Hafiz

Chapter 9

Tipping Point

The fourth place of power is the tipping point. The idea of a tipping point has been repeatedly expressed, from Gebser, to Graves and Wilber, to global risk assessment. It was popularized by Malcolm Gladwell's best-selling book in 2000, *The Tipping Point: How Little Things Can Make a Big Difference*. At the tipping point, an idea suddenly takes hold and becomes popular or accepted. Picture a straw on a table that you keep nudging toward the edge; the tipping point for that straw is the final nudge that sends it over the edge. It can be reversible or, like breaking a glass of wine, irreversible. A tipping point occurs when an idea, trend, or social behavior crosses a threshold and becomes generally and legally accepted, like same-sex marriages. How did the *Harry Potter* books written by an unknown author suddenly become wildly popular with children (and adults)? Cell phones, for example, were a luxury, until suddenly their use spread like wildfire all over the world. The environmental tipping point may have already been passed with immediately irreversible consequences, such as polar ice cap melting and global warming. The tipping point may turn Earth into a different planet from the one we're familiar with.

I was excited to find a study by scientists at Rensselaer Polytechnic Institute called "Minority Rules: Scientists Discover Tipping Point for the Spread of Ideas."[37] Using computational and analytical methods, the researchers showed that when just 10 percent of the population holds an unshakable belief, that belief will always be adopted by the majority of the society. Here is a source of power: if 10 percent of the world advocated the Tier 2 values (which incorporate Tier 1 values), a multidimensional, integral approach would become possible, and a globally cooperative approach to risk management and issues could be adopted.

> Never doubt that a small group of thoughtful, committed citizens can change the world; indeed, it's the only thing that every has.[38]

One example of a local project that has had far-reaching effects is Story Bridge, founded by Dr. Richard Geer. Using his techniques, project leaders bring together people of all ages to share their personal stories. These are winnowed and arranged to tell a larger story of the community and then enacted for audiences of locals and visitors, thus empowering both individuals and the group. Inspired, the group develops action plans for community change. Story Bridge has brought change, hope, and redefinition to communities from eastern Kentucky to Beijing. After a quarter century, it remains a cultural and economic icon in Colquitt, Georgia, where the process began.

Examples of other positive ventures span a wide range. Many start with thinking globally and acting locally. Some examples include legislative changes, church-sponsored gardens to feed the homeless, tiny homes for homeless veterans, educational support for the disadvantaged, and start-up funds for microbusinesses.

Chapter 10

As Within, So Without

The last, most potent place of power we have is changing within. External reality is a reflection of our inner world. If we change our perceptions, then we change our external reality.

> When we are no longer able to change a situation, we are challenged to change ourselves.[39]
>
> —Viktor E. Frankl

> Seeing is not believing; believing is seeing! You see things, not as they are, but as you are.[40]
>
> —Eric Butterworth

Of the millions of things that stream by every second that we could pay attention to, we grab about 134 bits of information, of which most people can consciously recall five to nine. These then create our reality. What we pay attention to depends on what interests us, what we believe, what our past experiences have been, the culture we grew up in, the language we speak, and the like. A politician would be paying attention to polls, news, focus groups, and public opinion. A mother would pay attention to her family's diet and her child's health, sleep patterns, and cries for help. A mystic might be attuned to inner vision, intuitive senses, and divine love.

What we pay attention to creates our reality. It determines what we think the world is or how we think it should be. We form our beliefs and values from that to which we pay attention. What we pay attention to also determines our internal state, such as our emotions and our physical responses to the external world. Those form our behaviors and attitudes, which largely determine what comes back at us from the external world. And the cycle continues. In other words, how we perceive the world is projected onto the world as our reality. To change external events, go within, where first we created our reality. Psychiatrist Iain McGilchrist has this to say:

> For one thing, whatever we know, we cannot know what it would be like in the absence of our knowing it, and different people find different things in the world. Even the same person finds different things on different occasions, when the context or the type of attention changes. That does not mean, of course, that everything that exists owes its nature and existence solely to us. But it does mean that, whether we are scientists or not, we can only know the world as we have inevitably shaped it by the nature of our attention.[41]

Part Two
Internal Change

> If you change yourself, you have already
> started to change the world.[42]
>> —Osho

To say that the world is undergoing rapid change is something of an understatement. Daily we witness this change. The institutions—religious, financial, political, ecological, and societal—that have formed the underpinnings of societies for centuries are crumbling. As we witness the collapse of the old world, we observe a simultaneous, parallel birth of the new. As the brilliant Indian writer, poet, and activist Arundhati Roy so eloquently wrote: "Another world is not only possible, she is on her way. On a quiet day, I can hear her breathing."[43]

With the many changes happening in our outer world, there are major changes happening in our inner world as well. There is a clear bridge between the two.

> There are times when we stop, we sit still. We listen and
> breezes from a whole other world begin to whisper.[44]
>> —James Carroll

It is incumbent on us both individually and collectively to understand and harness the inner so that we can intelligently, with wisdom, meet the outer world changes. Can we, as Arundhati Roy suggests, hear the breathing of our new world and of ourselves? We are birthing the new, even though none of us really knows what the new is. We are developing the blueprint daily. We are gestating it, like a baby in the womb.

> The future that our hearts tell us is possible—the future that is not a mere continuation of the past—comes from heeding our own soul's calling and how that calling responds to the call of life.[45]
>
> —Ria Baeck and Helen Titchen Beeth

> Though the forces of entropy and fear seek to contain or regress us, we know that there is no going back. Our complex time requires a wiser use of our capacities, a richer music from the instrument we have been given. The world will thrive only if we can grow. The possible society will become a reality only if we learn to be the possible humans we are capable of being.[46]
>
> —Jean Houston

"True change is within;
leave the outside as it is."
-Dalai Lama

Photograph by Ron Cordek

Most of us live lives of habituation. Normally we tend to think the same thoughts, have the same reactions, go down the same rabbit paths of thought patterns. This tends to give us the same outcomes—the same problems, the same types of friends, the same levels of finance, and the same patterns of life. If you keep the same attitude, you can leave behind a bad relationship or a incompatible job and re-create them elsewhere; nothing changes but the stage set.

> Your beliefs become your thoughts,
> Your thoughts become your words,
> Your words become your actions,
> Your actions become your habits,
> Your habits become your values,
> Your values become your destiny.[47]
>
> —Mahatma Gandhi

When we separate from our thoughts and become aware enough to observe them, we stand in a witness place, noticing them rather than running after or resisting them. By slowing down the automatic, habitual mind chatter, we gain access to a deeper place, a portal through which imagination and creativity can come. This is much more profound than the mind's usual stream of consciousness.

> The chains of habit are generally too small to be felt until they are too strong to be broken.[48]
>
> —Samuel Johnson

The unconscious mind has ideas about who we are, what we believe, and what we expect, and it gives them to us every day; even different jobs or people result in the same issues and patterns. To transform our lives, we need to go into the operating system of our brains and get our unconscious minds to make the necessary adjustments. When we persuade our unconscious minds to change, our lives will change.

> The Mind: a beautiful servant, a dangerous master.[49]
>
> —Osho

Changing within is taking the blindfold off the habitual, automatic roles we take on, our beliefs about ourselves, and the limitations we think we have. It's about reshaping ourselves into whom we came here to be.

Photograph by Katherine Battenberg

Sugar and spice
and everything nice
that's what little girls are made of
 So she put in a hand
 and pulled out a gland
 and said, "What a strange girl am I."[50]
   —Excerpt from "What the Little Girl
    Did" by Roger McGough

Three Simple Guidelines

For years I've adopted three simple guidelines to help me navigate life changes. I invite you to use them as you go through the rest of *Change Within, Change the World.*

Guideline 1: Life Is a Point of View
Change your point of view, and you can change your life.

Photograph by Jane Battenberg and Ron Cordek

Your point of view about things acts like a magnet, drawing that reality to you and in a sense manifesting it for you. If you think people are generous, they will be. If you think people can't be trusted, they won't be.

> There is nothing either good or bad, but thinking makes it so.[51]
>
> —William Shakespeare

Take a look at your automatic, often unconscious beliefs about how things are. You can examine your life in general, the things that always seems to happen to you. Or focus on a specific subject, such as money, intimacy, parents, men/women, your abilities, fate or luck, God, or work. Quickly write in a stream-of-consciousness[52] way what you think about that subject in relationship to you personally. It's *your* life, so describe *your* point of view.

Next, rewrite each point of view to be the most powerful, positive viewpoint anyone could have. For example:

- I can't seem to ever get ahead.
  Rewrite: I expect to get ahead and be outrageously successful.
- God lets me down.
  Rewrite: God loves me and has my back.
- People will cheat me if given a chance.
  Rewrite: People are surprisingly helpful and generous to me, even when I don't expect it.

You can consciously adopt a different point of view as an experiment to see how the world shapes to conform to that new viewpoint. Once, on a group trip, one of the participants was particularly biting and cruel toward me for no apparent reason; she frequently made derisive comments about me to the entire group. I decided to adopt the point of view that she was a very good friend and really liked me. Whenever I saw her, I greeted her as if we were great buddies. She began going out of her way to do nice things for me and to hang out with me. We stayed good friends for many years after.

Your experiment is to adopt a new point of view about yourself, a situation, how things turn out, people in general, or whatever you choose. Apply the Rule #1/Rule #2 to it:

Rule #1: I always succeed.
Rule #2: If I don't succeed, revert to Rule #1.

If I had failed in my first attempt to turn the woman on the tour into a friend, I would have tried another approach, and if that didn't work, I would have persisted, implementing one strategy after another until I did succeed. Keep this point of view and see what changes. Life is a point of view. If you don't like what is happening, change your point of view about it.

> Find ecstasy in life; the mere sense of living is joy enough.[53]
>
> —Emily Dickinson

Photograph by Ron Cordek

Guideline 2: It's All Practice

Just as a baby learning to walk needs to fall down many times in order to learn to run, it's important to give yourself permission to keep practicing until you learn the skill or get the outcome you want. Drop the need to do things right in favor of adopting the "it's all practice" rule.

> Learn from the mistakes of others. You can't live long
> enough to make them all yourself.[54]
> —Eleanor Roosevelt

The value of this rule is illustrated by a well-known story about the famous hypnotherapist Dr. Milton Erickson. Asked if he ever failed to get results with his patients, he replied that he never failed, although he was still working on some of his patients. You've heard the old adage "If at first you don't succeed, try, try again." Often, when the things we try don't work or don't turn out the way we'd like, we make a judgment about ourselves, vowing something like, "I'll never do that again!" We give up rather than think of a different approach or practice to become more skillful. One of the presuppositions of NeuroLinguistic Programming (NLP) is that "the person or element with the most flexibility in a group or system will have the most influence."[55] Imagine a mother whose screaming child is lying on the floor in a grocery store demanding candy. The only way the mother can quiet the child is to acquiesce to the child's demands. Now imagine that mother lying down on the floor next to the child throwing her own temper tantrum, screaming that she *won't* give any candy! Bet that child never tries that again! The example may be a little outrageous, but it demonstrates the idea that the more flexible you can be and the more behaviors you can practice, the more you learn and the more control you have over your life.

Where in your life have you given up because you weren't good enough, or you didn't succeed at first, or it was easier to do it someone else's way? In each situation, imagine how being flexible and trying different behaviors can produce an outcome you like.

For a week, adopt the rule that "It is all practice." If you ask your boss for a raise and she says no, think of different approaches and keep trying. Demonstrate how valuable you are to the team, for example, by suggesting new ways of doing things. If you feel bad because you didn't do something well, put your chin up, remind yourself that it's just practice, and keep practicing.

Guideline 3: Keep It Fun
The elements of simplicity and playfulness can hold your attention more than lengthy diatribes, so make it enjoyable.

> Life is a Celebration. Don't analyse it, celebrate it![56]
> —Osho

Seeing the humor in a situation can lighten the mood and lead to more innovative resolutions. Often we can make something very complex that doesn't need to be. Profound spiritual truths are simple. On the other hand, intellectual pursuits, such as planning, organizing, and categorizing ideas, require complexity.

> Life is a playground and a laboratory; avoid neglecting one for the other.[57]
> —T. F. Hodge

The Ground on Which You Stand

Before beginning the work of inner change, you need to identify how you envision the world you want and what you're willing to do to bring it into being. This is the ground on which you stand.[58]

It is this partnership—imagination and action—that creates your world. The following section provides a template for clarifying your thoughts and intentions. There are three parts: "My Ideas," in which you describe your beliefs and your dreams; "My Imagination," in which you play with your ideas, as wildly as you dare, to create something you long for; and "My Actions," in which you commit to, or at least describe, the deeds necessary to bring your dream into being. Using the techniques presented there, you can delve beneath the surface to the deeper issues that make up your ground of being.

My Ideas
What kind of world do I want to live in, where my heart and soul feel alive, where I am living authentically, bringing the gifts I came into this life with and offering them to our world?

We are sacred artists, painting our lives on the canvas of the universe.

Art by Bridget Reynolds

Your fantasies define you, so dream carefully. A man with no imagination is a man with no future in today's world—and no past in tomorrow's.[59]

—Jarod Kintz

Picture a world that you would like to live in. Spend some time describing in detail this world, its ecology, education system, housing, fiscal system, interlinking of ethnic groups, societal governance, resources, food, water, and the like. You may first describe your ideal world in prose, poetry, or song. Or make a mind map of each category.

Use art to express this world. Draw. Sculpt. Create a storyboard or collage of pictures, sketches, or other visual expressions.

Read poetry to express your ideas—poetry often enriches ideas first expressed in prose. Write a poem about it. Sing a song to give life to your ideal.

Play music you like to dance to, and then express, in dance and movement, the feelings of living authentically.

A suggestion to deepen this exercise comes from the book my sister and I wrote, *Eye Yoga: How you see is how you think*. Use a patch[60] to cover your left eye as you continue to flesh out the details. By patching the left eye, you are artificially enhancing your left-brain activity. For example, you may find yourself creating procedures and rules (a left-brain activity). Next, patch your right eye to enhance your right-brain, creative, emotional, whole-system approach.

My Imagination

Can I take a blank canvas and paint this world with my imagination? Buckminster Fuller always started with the biggest picture he could envision before designing anything, even something as mundane as a toilet. So, let your imagination soar as you picture the world you want to create and live in.

> Everything in the world of soul has a deep desire and longing for visible form; this is exactly where the power of the imagination lives.[61]
>
> —John O'Donohue

Art by Bridget Reynolds

Imagination is not only the unique human capacity to envision that which is not, and, therefore, the foundation of all invention and innovation. It is arguably the most transformative and revelatory capacity.[62]

—J. K. Rowling

How far will your imagination stretch in envisioning the kind of world you would like to live in? Let your imagination soar as you envision the world you want to create and live in.

Review what you have created. Where have you just recreated something you are already familiar with? Where have you gone outside the box to envision something truly different? Where were you held back by such thoughts as *Well, that can never happen* or *That's not possible?*

If you could have *anything*, what would you design?

Where were you recreating what you are familiar with? What can you imagine beyond *that?*

Use your talents to envision new possibilities you haven't yet dared to dream.

My Actions
How willing am I to manifest this, and how long could I sustain such a dedication to action?

> You must give everything to make your life as beautiful
> as the dreams that dance in your imagination.[63]
> —Roman Payne

> If you want to change the world, throw a better party![64]
> —Rick Ingrasci

"The meaning of life is to find your gift. The purpose of life is to give it away."
- Pablo Picasso

"She let her words fly forth as blessings, like white birds cheering the heart." —Denise Kester

In Hank Wesselman's book *The Bowl of Light*, native Hawaiian kahuna Hale Makua advised a gathering that each individual has the potential as well as the responsibility to become a world redeemer. "Each of us must become the change that we wish to experience. There simply is no other way. If we wish to create a new and better world, we must dream our world into being ... and then we must act on our dreams to bring them into manifestation through ourselves."[65]

In light of that wisdom from Hale Makua, take some time to reflect on your purpose in life. As you ponder your particular gifts and skills, as well as the life lessons you are here to learn, apply these things to your role in dreaming into being the change you wish to experience. Before you can ascend into creative action in the world, it is important to descend into yourself to know the truth of who you really are.

> Be patient with yourself. Self-growth is tender; it's holy ground. There is no greater investment.[66]
> —Stephen Covey

Section III

Developing Skills

In this section you will practice stretching your thinking to give you tools to do the change work in later sections. It's not about getting things right; it's about practicing the skills. So consider this section a workbook to improve your skills. Of course, you will be working on yourself and your life in the process, so you may find that changes occur as a result. But since it is just practice, feel free to experiment, explore, and try new things.

At the end of each chapter there is a "Treasure Hunt" section where you can deepen your work with the topic. By delving into it, using your own life experiences and issues, you are hunting for treasures of insights and ways to reframe your life: how you see things, and new directions, skills, powers, and resources. Doing the suggested processes can bring the book alive for you personally.

Chapter 11

What's Really Important

There was this man standing head to toe with a lamppost, pushing and struggling against it, trying in vain to move forward. A passerby asked him what he was doing. He said, "I'm trying to get home, but this dern lamppost is in my way!" Have you ever felt like you were struggling against some monumental problem or emotion that was as unyielding as a lamppost?

In a visit to my family, I found myself pulled back into old childish reactions that didn't reflect the current me at all. I was up against that dern lamppost! I wanted to re-create myself, to pull myself up by my bootstraps out of that old muck, but how?

The very questions we ask ourselves are steps that can lead us away from or around a problem—or take us even deeper into it. So, how is this useful in getting around that dern lamppost that we keep metaphorically running into?

When you are caught up in a problem or emotion, you are really bogged down in the details of it with no big-picture perspective. To move to a bigger perspective, you can ask the following questions:

- What's my higher purpose for this?
- What's my ultimate intention?
- What is this problem an example of?

The man struggling with the lamppost forgot that his intention was to get home so he could kick off his shoes and relax. He was so engrossed in pushing against it that he couldn't step back to see that he only had to walk around it in order to get on with his original purpose. By asking these big-picture questions, he remembered his intention for his daily actions; he could step back to see space around the problem (the lamppost), and this gave him more options.

When I was immersed in my old childhood reactions to my family, I asked myself what my real purpose was in being with them. As I remembered I was there to share love and support with them, my negative emotions lifted. Evoking this higher purpose for our family interactions dissolved my childhood reactions.

By using these simple yet powerful questions, we can gain the perspective needed to see our way around problems and sort out which details are important. Business partners who can't even agree on the wallpaper color for their office can agree that their purpose for the business is to make a profit. Concentrating on profit makes the wallpaper issue inconsequential. Focusing on our vision, our highest intention, keeps us from being sidetracked into wasteful, useless minutiae or negative emotions that don't align with our overarching purpose.

Here is a powerful meditative exercise: For one day, for everything you do, every thought you think, every feeling you have, ask yourself the following questions:

- What is my purpose for this?
- What is my highest intention?

When you go to the grocery store, ask what your purpose is. To get food, of course. Food for what purpose? To give you energy and keep you alive. Energy and aliveness for what purpose? So you can do the work you are here for. That may lead you to buy fresh vegetables instead of cookies. By constantly questioning everything in your daily life, you may find dramatic shifts, new solutions, even a renewed sense of purpose and spirituality. Take yourself off automatic and look at everything through these powerful yet simple questions to re-create yourself in alignment with your highest purpose.

Treasure Hunt

This exercise, the Hierarchy of Ideas, is taken from NLP techniques.[67] It involves moving a topic on a scale, up (greater abstraction), down (greater detail), and across (other examples). By making this a daily practice, you can expand your mind's ability to reflect on many aspects of an idea. Let's see what this looks like when we use baseball as an example. First move it up the hierarchy scale by asking what it is an example of.

- Baseball is an example of sports.
- Sports are an example of exercise.
- Exercise is an example of movement.
- Movement is an example of aliveness.

Now move laterally on the scale. If baseball is one example of sports, what are other examples? You might offer tennis, golf, basketball, and soccer. You have thus broadened the context of baseball as a sport.

Next move down on the hierarchy scale by going into more detail. Different types of baseball include softball, hardball, slow and fast pitch, and hot bats and wood bats. The baseball teams can be girls, boys, coed, men, women, recreational, or minor and major leagues. Major leagues can be American or National. National League includes Atlanta Braves, Chicago Cubs, LA Dodgers, Saint Louis Cardinals, Philadelphia Phillies, Washington Senators, and Pittsburgh Pirates. You can go into more detail on the Philadelphia Phillies by naming their team members.

By taking anything—an idea, an object, an activity, an emotion—up and down the hierarchy scale, you gain facility and flexibility in your thinking. You stretch your brain and expand your thinking beyond your habitual boundaries. Applying these techniques to a wide variety of areas, from sales to education, from directing a dialogue to structuring an overall plan, includes these benefits:

- Moving up the scale helps to identify the highest purpose for things, gives a category for things below it, and creates agreement and alignment.
- Moving down the scale fleshes out details and identifies distinctions and differences. By bringing out many points of view, disagreements can enrich the conversation.
- Moving laterally on the scale gives more examples within the category and broadens its context.

Just for practice, take five things up, across, and down the hierarchy scale. Do it until you get the idea and can do it with ease. Once you have this skill, you are ready to apply it in a more practical way.

Practice 1

Choose a topic or issue that is controversial, a disagreement between you and your partner, for example, about where to take your vacation. You want to relax by the seashore and read books. He wants to do something active like hiking the Grand Canyon or scuba diving in Cozumel. Before you get into a knock-down, drag-out, move up the hierarchy scale to the place where you agree: you want to take your vacation together, and you both like the outdoors. Then move back down the scale into the details, remembering the agreements you arrived at going up the scale, and work out a plan. It might be going to some place by the sea where you can relax on the beach and he can scuba dive.

Practice this until you are comfortable with the concept of moving up the scale until you agree and then moving back down into the details, keeping in mind that you do, in fact, agree.

Practice 2

Take a journal with you as you go through a day. Ask yourself, and write in your journal, what your purpose is for everything you do. Consider how you spend your time, whom you choose to talk with, what food you buy, what news you listen to or read, and even how you drive your car. Ask yourself the purpose of each activity. And what is the purpose for that? And its purpose? Examine one day to extract your highest purpose for everything. At the end of the day notice the deeper patterns you discovered. Did you spend a lot of your time, thought, and energy on relatively unimportant things, or were you aligned with your purpose?

Practice 3

Identify something you want to change or gain new solutions for. Run it up and down the scale until you get new insights. First, identify your topic. It could be anything, such as wanting to lose weight, desiring to travel, or selling more of your artwork.

Lose Weight

Going up the scale: I want to lose weight. Lose weight for what purpose? (For health, to look good.) And what is the purpose of that? Keep going up until you extract your highest purpose.

Going laterally: I want to lose weight. Losing weight is one example of living healthily. What are other examples of living healthily?

Going down the scale: I want to lose weight. Specifically how much weight do I want to lose and in how much time? Do I have a plan for losing this weight?

Travel

Going up: I want to travel. For what purpose? To experience and learn from other cultures. Experience and learn for what purpose? To connect with people and understand them in a deeper way. Keep going until you find what deeper purpose is driving this desire.

Going laterally: I want to travel. Travel is one example of visiting areas where I haven't been. What are other ways to visit areas I haven't been to?

Going down: I want to travel. Specifically which places would I like to travel to? How long would I like to travel? How often? Do I have a budget?

Sell More Artwork

Going up: I want to sell more of my artwork. Sell more for what purpose? To bring in more income. And what's the purpose of that? To allow me to purchase more art supplies so I can create more artwork.

Going laterally: I want to sell more of my artwork. Selling more is an example of my work being better known. In addition to selling more, what other ways can my work become better known?

Going down: I want to sell more of my artwork. Specifically which of my art pieces do I want to sell? For what price (raise or lower the price)? How much is more, and by what amount would I like my sales to increase?

Chapter 12

But I Have No Choice!

We don't get to choose what is true. We only get to choose what we do about it.[68]

—Kami Garcia

How many times and in how many different circumstances have you heard someone say—or perhaps you've even said it yourself—"But I have no choice"? You might feel helpless in light of overwhelming odds. Or perhaps the grip of a strong emotion is tumbling your equilibrium. Obligations, financial difficulties, or even opposition from family can present viselike constrictions to your freedom of choice. These situations create tremendous disempowerment, feelings of being trapped, of being a victim, with no available options.

Feeling like there's no way out can drain your spirits, your motivation, and your creativity. Once you give yourself over to having no choice, you move into victimhood. Victims can't do anything about it, so they just give up and quit looking for solutions. When they surrender their self-esteem and response-ableness (ability to respond), their physical and emotional health can begin to reflect the situation.

A client found herself in a dilemma. On the one hand, she was desperate to retire. On the other, she was unwilling to bring the matter up to her husband. She knew that cancer was her way out of this double bind; she confessed she would rather die than talk to him. And she did. Shakespeare's phrase "hoist with his own petard"[69] uniquely fits this situation of victimhood. You might call it shooting yourself in your own foot.

When you experience a strong negative emotion, like anger, depression, or fear, over which you feel you have no control, what can you do? The title of Susan Jeffers's book *Feel the Fear and Do It Anyway* expresses one approach. Recently I accidentally erased seven hours of inspired writing on my computer—gone. Gone were those carefully crafted expressions from the Muse of Writing. I felt such helpless anger and loss, and there was nothing I could do about it. I tried to re-create the work, but the well was dry. I tried to cry, but instead a fierce determination arose to get the job done even if it wasn't as beautifully crafted. I made an appointment with myself for several days later to redo it, to allow my unconscious plenty of time to get ready. I invoked all the help I could think of, and the work was recreated, albeit not with the fluidity of the first writing. Curiously, however, it left me with an unexpected sense of power; the work was inside me in some visceral way that couldn't be destroyed. In the long run, realizing that was worth more than the beautiful lost words.

To evaluate two boys, a psychiatrist left them in separate rooms. The pessimistic boy was surrounded by the latest toys. The optimistic one was put in a room full of horse manure. When the psychiatrist returned to the pessimistic child an hour later, he was crying. Several of the toys had broken, he didn't know how to operate others, and soon he'd have to leave these fancy toys behind. Shaking his head, the psychiatrist headed for the optimistic child's room. This tyke was whistling as he tossed the manure. When asked what he was doing, he gleefully replied that with all that manure, there was bound to be a pony in there somewhere, and he was going to find it!

Adopting the attitude that there must be something one can do or some point of view that would shift the emotions gives energy, empowerment, and creativity to the situation. That is the key to moving out of victim mode. It is an inside job.

Supporting the point of this anecdote are studies by cutting-edge cell biologist Dr. Bruce Lipton, who breaks our outmoded Newtonian flat-earth mentality concerning what affects our physical body in his book *The Biology of Belief.* He writes, "The notion that only physical molecules can impact cell physiology is outmoded. Biological behavior can be controlled by invisible forces, including thought, as well as it can be controlled by physical molecules like penicillin."[70] Further, he says, "Genes and DNA do not control our biology. Instead DNA is controlled by signals from outside the cell, including the energetic messages emanating from our positive and negative thoughts."[71]

In the end, keeping choice in our lives is critical to keeping ourselves healthy. Our very cells respond to our thoughts. Rather than being the victim of circumstances over which we seemingly have no control, we can reach for the grit and strength to change our attitude. It's not always easy, but the stakes are high as we look for the pony that's got to be somewhere in all that manure.

Treasure Hunt

Practice moving from a no-choice outlook to creating choices.

> "Would you tell me, please, which way I ought to go from here?"
> "That depends a good deal on where you want to get to," said the Cat.
> "I don't much care where—" said Alice.
> "Then it doesn't matter which way you go," said the Cat.
> "—so long as I get *somewhere*," Alice added as an explanation.
> "Oh, you're sure to do that," said the Cat, "if you only walk long enough."[72]
>
> —Lewis Carroll

> "It is our choices, Harry, that show what we truly are, far more than our abilities."[73]
>
> —J. K. Rowling

> Sometimes you have to choose between a bunch of wrong choices and no right ones. You just have to choose which wrong choices feel the least wrong.[74]
>
> —Colleen Hoover

Choice is a tricky thing. When you move from thinking there's nothing you can do and it's out of your hands to taking responsibility for a choice, it may not be easy. Sometimes you must choose the lesser of two evils. Sometimes you can choose an uncomfortable option for a better ultimate outcome. Sometimes you have to shift how you view the situation, like expecting to find a pony in there somewhere. To practice developing the skill of moving from no-choice to choice thinking, you will need examples of where you feel you have no options, where you feel it's out of your control. Don't worry about whether your examples are inconsequential or monumental; it is all practice.

To help compile your list of where you feel stuck with no options, consider these responses:

- It's not my fault.
- There's nothing I can do.
- Why me?
- This always happens to me no matter what I do or how I try to prevent it.
- It's out of my hands.
- Just bad luck.
- Nobody told me.
- There's no way out.
- What else can I do?
- Now I'm really in a bind!
- Darned if I do, darned if I don't.
- Now what?

Once you get a nice list to practice with, take each one through the following process. Even if you don't like the choices you come up with, you are training your mind (Puppy Training 101) to think you have choices and to keep coming up with options until you get really juicy ones you like!

1. You don't see any way out, but if you were to see options, what would they be?

    When faced with two equally tough choices, most people choose the third choice: to not choose.[75]
    —Jarod Kintz

2. Since not everyone would feel the same stuckness, ask what someone else would do in this situation. What would someone you look up to do?

3. You may not be able to change the circumstances or the event, but you *can* change how you look at it. What other interpretation, side benefit, or realization might be gleaned from it?

4. When faced with a difficult choice, look at what you value in the long run and choose something based on that. For example, having a difficult honest conversation with someone might be uncomfortable for you and upsetting for them, yet you can still feel good about staying true to your deeply held value of honestly communicating.

    It's not hard to make decisions when you know what your values are.[76]
    —Roy Disney

5. Pleasing others may lead you off the path of being true to what you value and stand for. If you tend to people-please, it is good to remember that this includes pleasing yourself!

6. Rather than blame someone else or bad luck or fate, look for any way you can take back responsibility. If this happens to you, where might you be doing it to someone else? If a bird messes on your windshield, where are you messing up

someone else's life? You are looking for ways to take back your response-ableness.

> But until a person can say deeply and honestly, "I am what I am today because of the choices I made yesterday," that person cannot say, "I choose otherwise."[77]
>
> —Stephen R. Covey

7. You are looking for ways to view the situation that allow you to reclaim your power, that don't leave you feeling a victim of circumstances. It's not about blaming yourself. It's about creating new options, different viewpoints, and reframes. You want to take back your energy, your power, your ability to respond to the situation. September 11 was a terrible tragedy, yet for many people it was a call to return to valuing time with their family. That didn't change the tragedy, but it did reset their values to something positive.

Chapter 13

Spring Forward, Fall Back: Eternal Cycles

Remember: no mud, no lotus.[78]

—Thich Nhat Hanh

Twice a year for most of us, we move our clocks, both physical and biological, into or out of daylight saving time. It is a transition time and, as such, marks a shift. As daffodils, freesias, and narcissus begin popping up from the bulbs I planted last year, they remind me of thoughts planted yesterday that bloom into tomorrow's reality.

Recall the Greek myth of Persephone, goddess of springtime, daughter of the Great Earth Mother Demeter. For a moment, step into that role, into the body of a lithe, attractive, young woman. They call you Sef, short for Persephone. It's boring in the castle on such a warm spring day, so you decide to gather flowers in the meadow. A particularly attractive flower catches your attention, and you reach down to pick it. Suddenly you realize it's not a flower at all, but the tail of a huge hellacious beast, Hades, God of the Underworld. Oops—wrong flower! Uh-oh! He carries you down under the earth to his realm. As the sunlight of day fades, you descend deeper into the depths of despair. Losing all hope of rescue, you resort to the only thing left that can comfort you—eating! You accept a few pomegranate seeds, allowing the sweet sourness to assuage your depression.

Here in this dark underworld you are the queen, until one day you are surprised by a visit from a lawyer, sent by your mother, Demeter. "I've got some good news and some bad news," the lawyer announces. "The good news is that you can come back up to the world of happiness, sunshine, and friends. The bad news is, since you ate something here, you must return for part of each year to be queen of the underworld."

Back in your castle, as you journal about your experiences, you realize you are no longer purely godlike. Now you are caught in the human cycles of emotions, from sunlight to the underworld and back. There will always be cycles. The question is, will you focus on the sunlight or on the darkness? In a sense, our negative emotions are our own underworld, so it helps to remember that Persephone ended up doing good works during the times she was forced to spend in the underworld, helping lost souls. Emotions are magnetic in nature. If you are an angry person, you may attract into your life angry people or situations. Conversely, if you've blocked out any expression of anger, you will need to attract people who act it out for you. Once you've done some spring-cleaning on those emotions, you regain the choice of what to focus on.

Focus is a tricky thing. If I tell you not to think of a purple giraffe, you have to think of that Disney giraffe before you can erase the image. Your unconscious mind doesn't process negatives very well. Have you ever gone on a diet and all you focus on is *not* having food? Diets are doubly hard because you're really focusing on—delete the *not*—*having* food, which often causes you to eat more. How many times do you undo positive manifestations by saying what you do not want? The trick is, once we formulate the words, they become an unconscious suggestion. We can expect to cycle through positive as well as negative emotions—that's life. The questions are, where is our focus, and what experiences are we drawing to us? And, like Persephone, how do we use our underworld emotions to do good works?

Treasure Hunt
You are continuing to uncover the unconscious rabbit paths of thought that keep recreating the same results in your life. You are increasing your skill at observing your mind chatter in order to

bring this programming to the surface. Once you become aware of the unconscious thoughts that have been subtly running your life, you can consciously work on changing them. You are hunting for negative focuses and expectations in an area of your life where you would like some positive change.

Choose an area of your life where you want to see positive changes, where you have goals or desires to work on. Some areas to consider are relationships, career, finances, health, fitness, and spirituality.

Choose a goal you have in this area, and write about it. Describe in detail your desires, your action plans, and what will need to happen to bring it to reality. Let your mind go as you write a stream-of-consciousness description of your goal.

You may want to set this aside for a time. Then go back and reread it. As you read, notice if you have focused on what you want or don't want, circling any place where you have described what you don't want. Like Persephone, explore the underworld to find areas where your thoughts go to what you do not want or what you are denying.

Sometimes it is subtle, like desiring money to keep you from being poor. *Not* wanting to be poor is a negative thought that can keep you focused on being poor. Look at your goal to see if it contains any subtle negatives. What you don't want can drive your behavior toward the very thing you want to avoid.

Have you set a goal that will correct something negative that happened to you before? If you want a relationship where there is trust, is that because in a previous relationship you didn't have it? That would be another subtle negative.

Do you want something to cover up for your feeling inadequate or undeserving? Perhaps you want love because you didn't feel loved or wanted as a child. Or you want wild success and fame because you've always felt like a failure.

Once you have delved into your underworld of negative focus, you can begin to reimage any negative expression into what you do want, shifting your focus to the positive. You may have to do some inner work to reveal what is really underneath your goal.

> So, friends, every day do something that won't compute. ...
> Give your approval to all you cannot understand. ... Ask
> the questions that have no answers. Put your faith in two
> inches of humus that will build under the trees every
> thousand years. ... Laugh. Be joyful though you have
> considered all the facts. ... Practice resurrection.[79]
>
> —Wendell Berry

Chapter 14

Shah! Talk to the Hand 'Cause the Face Ain't Listening!

There comes a time when the mind takes a higher plane
of knowledge but can never prove how it got there.[80]
—Albert Einstein

"Would you go out with me?" "In your dreams!" How many times
have you wanted something that seemed so out of reach that you
could only get it in your dreams? Dreams—that cotton-candy stuff
that wisps in and out of our consciousness in paroxysms of pleasure
or gnarly nightmares, nattering nabobs of negativism or scintillating
sensualities of celestialism—form the otherworldly reality of our
unconscious. Dreamy stuff may seem plausible but nonsensical,
a stream of consciousness with emotional import that grabs our
attention and pulls us down under the surface of the conscious to
that underworld where reality is gestated.

The question then becomes whether it is a figment of your
imagination—"you must be dreaming"—or a place where you image
something into reality. Dr. Jean Houston talks about "the mediocrity
of having a diffident relationship to the genius of inner space."[81]
She passionately pleads with people to develop their inner lives so
that they can connect with their higher destinies and orchestrate
their moods of creativity. She distinguishes between imagination and
the imaginal world: Imagination is the reproduction and reordering
of already existing ideas. The imaginal realm, on the other hand,

produces (rather than reproduces) big-picture perspectives, new creations, new paradigms and patterns.

A friend who writes software told me about his experience with emerging patterns. He was contemplating thousands of lines of a software program when suddenly he saw a much simpler way to express it in only a few hundred lines. He was profoundly affected by the experience of such an elegantly simple solution popping into his awareness. Ever since, he has tapped into the ability to wait until a beautifully streamlined pattern emerges in his mind. Before that experience he thought he was just a programmer; now he knows he is a creative pattern maker with a unique ability.

The tip of an iceberg above the water is deceptively bland when compared to the vast beauty of the gigantic ice formation below. Like that, our unconscious minds hold vast caverns of potential and beauty when compared to our conscious, intellectual minds. In order to tap into that potential, we may explore the boundary between the two. What are you thinking just before you wake up in the morning? What are your first stirrings of awareness in this hypnopompic state? And right before you fall asleep, when your body is very still, where do you go? Have you watched a child as sleep begins to overtake him and his thoughts turn inward to the dream state? Eyes still open, the child becomes very still, as if already asleep. That is the hypnagogic state, the drowsy period between wakefulness and sleep. The hypnopompic is the mirror state, leading out of sleep. During both, fantasies and hallucinations often occur.

Waking and dreaming are naturally occurring states, and we constantly slip back and forth between them. What is important is to be able to go to that in-between place at will and to use that state to create what we want. Each of us has a unique way to enter the imaginal realm, whether it is meditation, daydreaming, visualization, or just spacing out. If your hand is your unconscious and your face represents your intellectual conscious state, how do you get the two to talk to each other?

Treasure Hunt

The skill to develop is to increase your facility in using the imaginal realm. One of the best ways to do this is to meditate. First, explore the ways you slip into the meditative imaginal realm. What time of day is most conducive for you to do this? Does it happen automatically, or do you perform a ritual to get to that state? What makes your mind chatter recede and allows the dream patterns to begin to emerge? I suggest writing down how you best move into this state as if writing down a formula or a set of instructions.

The next step is identifying the gestative seed to be cultivated. In order for you to use the imaginal realm instead of the imagination, identify where you want a new paradigm, a creatively powerful, innovative way of thinking, or a different way of looking at or solving issues. Set that as your intention, and then go into the trance state of the imaginal realm, allowing the Muse of Potentiality to communicate.

Each day for one week set aside time to explore the imaginal realm as your conscious and unconscious minds develop a relationship. Write down what happens each day. At the end, write up your conclusions, solutions, insights, shifts, and creations.

The complexity of our world seems to demand we go deeper in search of new paradigms. Will you be satisfied with a mediocre relationship with your inner dream world, or will you cultivate the genius of your inner space?

Chapter 15

Using Time to Transform

It's a poor sort of memory that only works backwards.[82]
—Lewis Carroll

While I was helping my dad chop wood, we broke the ax handle. As I hammered a new handle onto the ax, the hammer slipped and slammed into my hand, causing immediate pain and swelling. Using a technique from Serge King, world-famous shaman, author, and expert on Hawaiian Huna, I quickly reviewed the events leading up to the moment to resolve any emotional causes for hitting my hand. Next, I reran the sequence of events in my mind, but with a different outcome. I acted it out, raising the hammer and almost hitting my hand, this time feeling the relief of just missing it. It took about sixty times of reenactment before the pain, swelling, and black-blue disappeared completely. No more pain—as if it hadn't happened, all to the amusement of my dad!

Time is tricky. Five minutes in pain can seem like hours, but time flies when you're having fun. But what if you could actually use time to transform your life? Instead of being measured in absolute minutes and hours, and once gone never to come again, and instead of being concrete, set in stone, suppose time were as malleable as a child's modeling clay.

When you wake up in the morning, how do you know to be you? You have an entire history of memories—emotional experiences, schooling, learnings, beliefs, family history, body size, body experiences, and more. All those elements make up who you think you are. The unconscious mind takes everything as if it is now. If you are remembering something in the past, your unconscious is recreating the neurotransmitters, hormones, and peptides that were activated in your body then—now. If you go back and actively reimagine a new, positive version of a past event with full emotional investment, you change the way your body stores that memory, and you literally change who you are.

A woman with multiple personality disorder (MPD) had full-blown adult diabetes with one personality, as determined by a test of her blood sample. When she changed personalities, she instantly shifted to not having diabetes, as evidenced by an immediate blood test. Another patient was allergic to orange juice with one personality and not allergic with a second. Different personalities have even been known to have different eyesights.[83] In all cases the different memories, life experiences, and beliefs of one personality versus the other resulted in different physical conditions.

The same is true for the future. If you actively imagine something in the future turning out just as you'd like it, feeling all the emotional pleasures of it as if it is happening now, you are installing a program in your unconscious to give you that very thing. The unconscious knows it has already happened like that in the future, so it gears everything to that reality. One winter when I was ski patrolling, I had been paid in cash, which I received in a white envelope with only "Jane" written on it. It must have fallen out of my parka pocket, because at the end of the day it was gone. There was little chance of seeing a white envelope on white snow. Even if someone honest found it, how likely were they to know who Jane was? I intensely visualized someone finding it and returning it to me; I felt all the excitement, relief, and gratefulness I would feel when that happened. When I told people I'd lost the envelope, they expressed sorrow for my loss. But I'd say, "Oh no, someone will find it." Sure enough, the next day a patroller spied it by the patrol room door and returned it. And I felt all the excitement, relief, and gratefulness I had imagined! Events tend to form around imagined outcomes, just as iron filings are shaped by a magnet. Because of many experiences like that, both my own and my clients', I have adopted this maxim: "Active imagination plus emotional investment equals a different reality, whether past or future."

Turning to science for corollaries, we find that the observer not only influences the observed but also can determine what is observed by their expectations. If you expect to see a photon act as a wave of energy, it does. If you measure it as if it is a particle of matter, it is.

Recent scientific experiments demonstrate that experienced meditators can skew the results of an otherwise random (fifty-fifty chance) direction of photons. Additionally, provided no one has yet seen the results, the meditators can influence them after the experiment is complete. Called double-slit experiments, these studies have been extensively replicated.[84]

Perhaps there is a situation you didn't handle well. You may feel guilty, a little sad, maybe even resentful. You can go back in your mind to that situation with all the insights, increased wisdom, and perspective from the present and replay it, handling it better. Notice how good you feel about how it turns out this time, and bring that feeling to the present. It's as if you now have two histories of that event, which give you more behavioral choices in future situations. It's possible that with a little practice, this technique can be applied to global situations as well as to our own lives. All you've got is your mind. If the past and future are truly malleable, then you have a responsibility to make up your mind as you want it, or else someone will make it up for you.

Treasure Hunt

> Imagination is everything. It is the preview of life's
> coming attractions.[85]
>
> —Albert Einstein

This hunt will give you practice in changing future and past events by using time, your emotional investment, and your imagination.

Shaping the Future

This may be a little easier to do than reshaping a past event, so practice first on the future. Choose an event that hasn't happened yet for which you desire a certain outcome, no matter how improbable. Make a video in your mind with yourself as the main actor.

1. In your video, this event turns out exactly as you want. See specifically when the event occurs, the place where it is happening, and perhaps the clothes people are wearing, the carpet color, the time of day, the weather—every detail as if you are there witnessing it unfolding just the way you desire.

2. Feel your feelings as the event happens. Intensify those positive feelings, amping them up. What are you saying, either to yourself or aloud? What are others saying?

3. Make the video as vivid and real as you can. It's all in your mind. And it's *your* mind, so make it mind as you envision this future event in your video.

4. Now step out of the video and watch it play as though you are viewing a movie of yourself in this future event.

5. Imagine your lifeline going from past to present to future. Float like a balloon above this lifeline and look down on it. If you can't see it, then sense or feel it or tell yourself what you are doing. Staying above your lifeline, go out in the future to the precise time where the event you videoed is happening. Insert your video into your future at that exact place. You may drop it in or watch it float or zoom down. Or you may sense that it locks in. Or you may say to yourself that you have inserted it. The way you insert it is your choice.

6. The instant the video is slotted in, feel or see every event from that future moment all the way back to the present as it rearranges itself to align with this future happening having occurred.

7. Now return to the present, installing into your lifeline between future and present the positive feelings of success you had at the event. Once you are back in the

present moment, you can just let things happen. You've already programmed the success. Let it happen. Let go of micromanaging and allow things to unfold. See what happens.

How close to your video did things turn out? Even if the details are different, the exercise keeps your mind creating positive outcomes, which is always a good practice. And if you get a green Porsche instead of a red one, it's close enough. Clients who have used this technique often report that they accurately envisioned the carpet in the room, the color of a dress, even the weather!

Reshaping the Past

Your unconscious mind stores your past in memory and from that forms beliefs about who you are, your limitations, how life is for you, what you are capable of, and so forth. Like the woman with multiple personalities who had diabetes with one personality and not with another, you create your present reality from your past. If you go back into the past to a specific event and gain a new perspective that allows you to experience it differently, you will have created a new memory with more resourceful responses. In a sense this is like updating your computer programming or creating a parallel reality. Your unconscious mind can't tell much difference between a real memory, which changes over time anyway, and an imagined memory with more behavioral and emotional resources. You have therefore given your unconscious mind more choice—to respond to situations with the limitations of your past or with the resourcefulness of your reenvisioned past. Given that choice, most unconscious minds will choose the past with more resources!

There are many techniques for going back into the past. One is to float above your lifeline to reframe a past event, using the steps described above in "Shaping the Future." In another method, borrowed from Dr. Jean Houston, you view your past, present, and future as an energetic wall of time and follow the wall back to the past event whose import you want to alter. Dr. Houston gives an example from her own experience: When she was a college student, a piece of theater scenery fell on her head, and she suffered a severe concussion, which seriously impaired her concentration and activity. She failed her classes, dropped her roles in major productions, and resigned as president of her drama group. It was a dark night of the soul. Later in life she traveled back on her wall of time to encourage and advise her younger self. She has a memory in the present of being visited in the past by a luminous being who encouraged her and told her things would get better in time.[86]

I tried this with my mother, who at ninety still remembered me at three years old breaking eggs and smearing them on our radio. She frequently told the story about how upset she was. Going back on the wall of time, I saw her showing me how to break the eggs into a bowl and make cookies. In this version she diverted a destructive behavior into a creative teaching experience! After I reenvisioned the experience, Mom never told that story again, and I had the pleasure of remembering her supporting my creativity.

To practice this, choose an incident from the past that you wish would have turned out differently or about which you want to alter your feelings. Go back on the wall of time to the event and reenvision it as a positive experience.

Creating Change—Temporal and Atemporal Alternation

Temporal refers to events that occur at a specific time. Atemporal means independent of time. A series of temporal events can create a gestalt, that is, a collection of feelings that have been fused in the mind as one experience.

Here is an example of the way a problem is created by a series of unrelated temporal events that come together in an atemporal condition that is greater than its discrete parts might suggest. A client and I tracked the development of this gestalt

When she was young, a bee (*zzzz*) stung her. That is a temporal occurrence, happening at a particular time. Later, a dog growled at her (*grrrr*); it didn't bite, but she was scared nonetheless, and the growl became connected to the bee's buzz. Years afterward, she associated the roar of a plane's engine (*brrrr*) with the prior scares and developed a terror about flying. Even though she no longer remembers the specific events, they have formed a generalized phobia triggered by the similar sounds—the gestalt has morphed into a dread of flying. This is atemporal, existing out of linear time. It is not created by a single event but grows out of a series of incidents that the unconscious mind has merged into a single experiential feeling.

Systemic properties of the whole are destroyed when a system is dissected into its isolated elements. In order to change the gestalt (in this case, the phobia), it is necessary to recover the first event. Going back in time to a specific event is temporal. By doing so, you are breaking the gestalt down into the parts exclusive to that event and thereby uncoupling the phobia. In our example, recovering the sound of each scary event and reframing the fear allows the phobia of flying to disappear.

The framework for change is the alternation between temporal and atemporal, as follows:

- Name the generalized unwanted feeling (gestalt)—atemporal.
- Go back in time to the first specific event of the feeling—temporal.
- Go before the first event and reframe the situation—atemporal.
- Come back into time (using the wall of time or your lifeline) and move forward from the first occurrence to the present, observing the changes that result from your reframed, expanded awareness—temporal.
- You have uncoupled the unwanted feelings and created a positive, generative replacement, a new gestalt—atemporal.

Section IV

Creating Personal Change

In section III you practiced the following:

- moving up, across, and down a scale of thinking from abstract to detail
- creating choices with possibility thinking
- shifting your focuses to positive from negative
- increasing your ability to imagine
- going backward and forward in time to create possible past and future events

In section IV you will be going deeper, building on the skills you developed in section III. It is about using beliefs, values, and mind-body wisdom to shape your reality.

- What you believe has a way of becoming reality—that is, you are what you believe you are. Beliefs are inner programs that keep you repeating the same patterns. They are the self-created hypnotic trances that your unconscious mind uses to define your reality.
- Just as your beliefs shape your reality, your words and imaginings act as powerful magnets to form your life

patterns. Becoming conscious of your inner-voice chatter gives you insight into what you are manifesting.

- Your most deeply held values determine your behavior, what you spend time and resources on, and how you evaluate yourself and others. Finding what you believe at the deep unconscious level gives you a powerful tool.

- Once you identify your values in the different areas of your life, you can get rid of what doesn't matter to you and create more time to spend on what is important. This gives you balance and harmony as you eliminate the unessential and the conflicts.

- If it's all in your mind, it's also in your body. Your cells are constantly eavesdropping on your every thought. Body conditions are usually a metaphor for unresolved emotional issues. Treating your body and your mind as one unit can bring healthy changes.

- Your body has an awareness and wisdom that your head isn't consciously aware of. Listening to your body takes trust and requires attention to subtle signals.

You've taken a big step toward developing the mental and emotional skills needed to do the deeper change work. Well done! In this journey, that is pivotal to taking the next step as you mine for the gold of change. This change work is not for the faint of heart. Your courage and self-honesty are paying off.

> Knowing others is wisdom; knowing the self is enlightenment.[87]
>
> —Tao Te Ching

Chapter 16

BYOB: Beyond Your Own Belief

> In religion and politics people's beliefs and convictions are in almost every case gotten second-hand, and without examination, from authorities who have not themselves examined the questions at issue, but have taken them second-hand from other non-examiners, whose opinions about them were not worth a brass farthing.[88]
>
> —Mark Twain

I was barely scraping by financially, living in a tiny apartment and scrimping wherever possible. In looking at my astrology chart, I could see not one but three triangles that formed a beautiful Star of David. I asked the astrologer what they might mean. After a hesitation, he said, "You'll never have to worry about money." My belief about money was that it was scarce and you had to work hard for it, yet the chart declared that it was always abundant for me. Back and forth I looked, puzzled and curious. Then it hit me. I could believe money was scarce, but since that belief went against my natural flow, it was much harder to create that reality. But I could do it if I wished. Or I could relax and let natural abundance come to me. I could have it either way, except one way was swimming upstream and the other was going with the flow. The only thing I needed to do was to change my belief about money. When I got that realization, I said, "Done!" Shortly after, a small piece of property I owned, which had been breaking even for many years, went way up in value, allowing me to sell it for more than the asking price. I bought my own home, and soon the flow of clients came more easily.

I don't take abundance for granted even today. But the experience of consciously deciding to change my belief about money and relaxing into a natural flow was profound!

Whom we believe ourselves to be is constantly changing. Before you learned to read, you weren't a reader. Until you learned to drive, you weren't a driver. "When I was a child, I spake as a child ... when I grew and became a man, I put away childish things."[89] We are continually morphing into new identities, new images of ourselves: a child, a rapper, a student, a teacher, a programmer, a marathoner, a grandparent, an elder.

Suppose for a minute that you are what you believe you are. Your belief acts as a program that runs your reality computer. Your belief is a template, a pattern that shapes your every experience, even your body. Well, if that is true, you may ask, how do I change my belief? We all get stuck in emotions and patterns that we'd rather not have. "I'm always the last one chosen for a team." "I always seem to attract men [or women] who use me and cheat on me and want me to take care of them." "I don't seem to have the enlightening spiritual experiences that other people do." "I'm no good at math." These patterns must be coming out of some unconscious belief, because we certainly wouldn't choose them consciously! They are technical difficulties beyond our control—maybe!

Imagine yourself with a lampshade over your head, trying to see where you are, and all you see is the inside of the shade. Or think of a stage hypnosis show where the hypnotist gets the volunteers to cluck like chickens and do other stupid things. That is what happens when we get stuck in the loop of a problem pattern. We are in a trance, meaning that even though we know better, we keep doing the same negative behaviors over and over again. Problems are trances, where we cluck like chickens and do stupid things. Like having a lampshade over our head, we think the problem is reality. We've been hypnotized into believing that it is who we are and the way things are. We don't know how to change the belief, the template, that negative pattern that we keep repeating.

Stephen Wolinsky, in *Trances People Live*, says this self-created hypnotic trance appears to *happen* to us, when in fact it is a deep-trance phenomenon that we create for ourselves.[90] Hypnosis is characterized by the shrinking, narrowing, and fixating of focus and attention, bypassing the conscious mind, and in the deep-trance phenomenon, we shrink our world down until we identify with our problem, thinking it defines us. The moment we become our problem, we cannot see other options and lose perspective, choices, and other resources. Once we shrink so far that we become the belief (problem), we are completely isolated inside that belief. "I'm not good enough." "I'm a loser." Anything you believe about yourself, anything you identify with, limits you by blocking out all other experiences or perspectives.

One way to regard this problem trance is as a small circle of limitation nested in a larger circle of unlimited possibilities. The way out of the small circle, the way to break the trance, is to step outside the boundary of the problem. Like pricking a balloon with a needle, once you get outside the problem, you destroy its boundary. When you can imagine a time before the problem existed (make it up), you have taken the lampshade off your head, and you can see new possibilities and new ways of being. You can create new beliefs that contain more possibilities. People in Christopher Columbus's time thought the world was flat and believed that if you sailed far enough, you would fall off the edge. Once they discovered the earth was round, they were no longer confined by the limitation of the flat-earth belief.

Here are some suggested ways for breaking the belief trance. Perhaps the very act of seeing your limiting beliefs as a hypnotic trance may help you choose to break them.

Go Before It Existed

First, feel the emotions and experience of your limiting belief. Then ask yourself to go back in time to before the limitation and emotions existed. Go as far back as you need to, even if it's to a time before you existed. When you arrive at the time before the belief existed, you have broken the trance.

Meditative State

Enter a meditative flow state that allows you to see yourself both without the limiting belief and with it. Notice all the choices you have without it.

Higher Help

Call on your spiritual support by whatever name you know it, higher self or guides, for example, to help you see a larger perspective. Invite it or them to help you reframe the situation that you believed described you.

The key point is that any limiting belief or problem is really a hypnotic trance where your whole identity is trapped within a narrow focus. That means you have blocked out other possibilities and perspectives. In reality, you are not your problems. When you change your beliefs and de-identify with your problems, you break the trance. It is as easy as making up a story about how it was before the problem ever existed. Good luck!

Treasure Hunt

To do the deeper work of breaking the hypnotic trance of your limiting beliefs, you will need to compile an inventory of your limiting identities to work with. Begin by describing your limitations and inadequacies. What can't you do well? What skills are lacking that hold you back? Take some time to get a long list, so you have plenty to practice with.

To start, choose one of the limiting beliefs from your list, one you *know* applies to you. Just to be sure it really is a limitation, list the ways you know that it is true.

"People take me for granted."
How do you know they do?

"They never call me; I have to call them. I don't get invited to parties. No one ever remembers my birthday. I always give gifts but don't get any in return."

How does it make you feel? Are you angry, sad, fearful, depressed, guilty? Where in your body do you feel it? Have you had this limitation all your life, or has it existed since some event or a certain age?

This process activates the neural networks of the problem in your body, lighting up the problem, making it viscerally real instead of merely an intellectual exercise. You need to know how the problem feels so you can compare that to how it feels when you don't have the problem. You can't get outside the problem until you can fully describe the experience of having it. Only then can you express what it would be to experience *not* having the problem.

Having lit up the experience of how the problem feels to you and how you know that you have the problem, the next step is to feel how it would be (or was) *not* to have that particular problem. For this you will need to use your imagination to go to a time when you did not experience the problem (limitation). If, for example, your limiting statement is "I feel isolated from everyone," go to a time before you felt isolated, a time when you felt you belonged. Go back as far as it takes to find this experience:

- early childhood
- a past life (make it up)
- an ancestor
- the beginning of time

The more deeply entrenched you are in identifying with your limitation, the more difficult it may be to go to a time before it existed. Let your mind make up a scenario that takes place before the limitation. Examples: "When I was in the womb, I didn't feel isolated." "Long ago in Rome, when I was a gladiator, I was surrounded by comrades."

Once you are past the limiting experience, describe to yourself how it feels: how your body responds, for example, what different thoughts you do or don't have, how relaxed or happy you are. Firmly anchor this experience in your being. Congratulations! You have just escaped the boundary of your limiting belief. Now come forward in time, bringing the insights and feelings of not having the limitation. Doing this may erase the former limitations you had. Or you may need to go back and forth between the two experiences a few times, learning from the process and discovering what caused the limiting belief in the first place. The whole experience of crossing between the two feelings erodes or erases the boundary between them, enabling you to let go of the limiting problem. When a pin pricks a balloon, the boundary and the balloon immediately disappear.

Once the limitation disappears, come forward in time, replacing your entire history with a new, better one in which the limiting belief doesn't exist. Think of updating your personal history this way as installing a new program on your computer. Or tell yourself that you're creating a parallel reality, a parallel memory line. Or even imagine that a snow plow is clearing the old limitations from your lifeline. Once you are back to the present, notice how you see yourself and notice your new abilities. Feel the differences. Look at how your life is now and how it will be different with your new beliefs about yourself. You will have gained insight into how the limitation was created and installed as well as how it might not have been real.

Chapter 17

The Power of Your Word

Words are living force. The words you use create your life.[91]

—Lailah Gifty Akita

Declaration, Creation, Manifestation

I had trained Kathy and her husband to be ski patrollers and had performed their marriage ceremony. When she was pregnant with her second child, she went to visit her dad. When I learned that her doctor had diagnosed a potentially serious condition called placenta previa, I placed my hands on her belly, silently connecting with the child. Then I said the words that came to me: "This condition will be gone in three weeks." A month later, Kathy's dad reminded me of that conversation and told me that her current doctor had told her he didn't know why the previous doctors had given the diagnosis, because there was no evidence at all of the condition. Having no conscious idea of why I had said the condition would disappear in three weeks, I was as amazed as my friends were at the power of the verbal declaration.

Some years ago I was skiing with a friend at Alta, Utah. Dark clouds were roiling overhead, and a heavy snowstorm was imminent. For our last run of the day, I suggested we ski down a mogul field (bumps). My friend pointed out that the light would be so flat that we wouldn't be able to see. Laughing, I declared that once we got to the bump run, the clouds would part and the sun would come out just long enough for us to ski down. As we neared the bumpy slope, my friend began to shout frantically. The storm clouds had opened to let the sun shine through just long enough for us to ski the slope safely. And then a heavy snowfall began.

Beliefs Shape Reality

An accountant friend always rechecked the restaurant bill for accuracy and usually found it was wrong by quite a bit. Alarmed, I began carrying a calculator to do the same, but the bill was usually right, and when it wasn't, it was often in my favor. The difference: he expected the bill to be wrong, and I expected it to be right.

One of my clients believed he was darkness, that there was a blackness in his heart, full of sadness and fear. All his life experiences bore this out, leaving him no choice, he thought, but to conclude that somehow at his core were darkness and nonlove, and his sole purpose was to suffer and sacrifice for God. His word, his belief, had become law in his life, a self-fulfilling prophecy that caused great suffering in his broken relationships. When at last he was able to entertain the idea that his belief came before his experiences and shaped them, he agreed to change his belief. Using Time Dimension Therapy techniques, he was able to go back to a time before conception when he was the light, one with God. He created a shaft of light that recalibrated his life experiences, obliterating the sadness and fear. His new decision about being light and peace at his core has now become the word, the law, in his life.

Words Evoke Images That Program Reality

We get what we declare and what we believe to be true or possible, but often we undo positive manifestations by making negative declarations, that is, by saying what we do not want. What do you want in a relationship? Well, I *don't* want a person who is (fill in the blank). How often do we tell someone what not to do? You're going to have an accident if you keep driving like that. You always talk too much, you're always late, you always lose your temper. What does a child do immediately after being told not to spill their drink? Oops— you guessed it! It takes a very conscious parent to phrase things positively rather than telling the child what not to do. Of course, we may start with describing what we don't want as a springboard to moving on to imaging what we do want. But unfortunately, once we image the words, they become an unconscious suggestion. When you read "Don't think of a yellow taxicab," the first thing you see is a yellow cab, and then you have to try to erase it from your mind.

The Power of the Word to Actualize the Potential

The boundary between two elements of an oscillating system seems to be where magic can occur.[92] The changing of the guard between breathing in and breathing out, that instant between taking in oxygen and releasing waste products, is one example. The pendulum shift from tick to tock, that split second when it is unclear whether the pendulum is moving in one direction or has started back in the other, is another. The boundary between potential and actual, between thinking of the creative possibility and actualizing it into form, is the magical place where one's belief, declaration, word, prayer, or decision can affect reality. This could be the key to actualizing thoughts. One day a friend's son, believing he could break the current swim record at a meet, knocked not just one or two but seven unbelievable seconds off his personal best. Rather than worrying if he was going to do well, he focused on his belief that he could swim faster than ever before—and he did.

The Moral of the Story

A man sitting under a bodhi tree was told that whatever he thought would be. So he wished for wealth, and he was wealthy. He conceived of a fine castle and had it. He imagined a beautiful wife and many wonderful children, and it came to pass. But he started worrying that it was too good to be true and perhaps he would lose his money, and he did. Then, seeing things go downhill, he worried that the peace in the land would not last, and war broke out. He wondered if his wife was unfaithful, and she was. He feared the plague, and it came. The moral of the story is that whatever we think might happen, will.

Our thoughts and our words have the power to become self-fulfilling manifestations or prayers.

Treasure Hunt

This is a tricky one to work with because you have to let go of your fears, your expectations, your judgments, and your thoughts about what is possible and probable. Enter into that magical place between potential and actual, and in your mind create what you envision happening. Play with it and see if you can do it. When it works, it's like magic. This is where you need your sense of the possible and of play. Since each person accesses this in their own unique way, your treasure hunt is to find your way and then replicate it. Find your own personal power in creating magic.

Chapter 18

What's Love Got to Do with It: Kite Strings, Values, Passion

Do you remember, perhaps from childhood, a person or a pet you loved dearly with all the passion and unconditionality that a child can feel? For some it was a grandparent or a favorite aunt or uncle. For others it was their dog and constant companion, or a "bestest" friend or first sweetheart. Think of something that you gave all your love to. Perhaps it was a place in nature, the woods, the ocean, your own private retreat. Maybe it was a passion for music or a sport— something you could immerse yourself in totally and forget time.

Those things that touched us deeply in our early years helped form us, gave us role models for more mature experiences of love, lit our way, and sustained, molded, and nurtured our souls. Just as the tiny kite string is essential for the beautiful kite to fly, these early experiences have enabled us to live with love and passion later in life. They have helped shape our values.

What we value determines how we spend our time, energy, and resources. If we don't value something, there is no motivation to do it. Have you ever procrastinated cleaning up a messy home, with *no* motivation to do it? It's only when something you value comes into play, like the opinion of visiting friends, that you are motivated to clean. No one likes to do their taxes, but eventually we value something else more, like a clean record or not having our bank account and wages garnished. At the deepest unconscious level, our values affect our behavior and our decisions and, after the fact, our evaluation of how well we did. Values are the kinesthetic, the feeling, the love, and the passion behind our behavior.

It is a fairly simple process to identify your values. First, choose an area of your life that you want to know more about, to discover what motivates you to behave certain ways. You may want to explore your relationships, your family, your work, or your health. Next, ask yourself (or have a friend ask you), "What's important to you in that area?" Ask that same question again and again, listing every response, noting your exact word(s). Do this quickly, so you don't have too much time to think about your answers, taking the first things that pop into your head. Your answers should be short, usually one word, such as *trust, compatibility, communication, freedom, respect,* and *chemistry.* Ask the question until you have run out of words. When this happens, pause to think, which will activate the deeper, more unconscious values. Often our most cherished values are taken for granted and emerge later. It can take several cycles for your most deeply held values to surface.

Continue until you have a list that sounds right, that feels good, that looks complete, usually about ten items, but it can be a much larger list. Next, rank the items, putting the number 1 by the value most important to you, the number 2 by the second most important, and so on. Then rewrite the list in numerical order. Now you can see the top three to five values that motivate you. If you chose career, for example, and income wasn't even on the list, you can see why you may be struggling financially. It's no wonder, since at the unconscious level money doesn't motivate you. You may see values that conflict, such as spending time with your family or friends versus needing freedom and alone time.

Looking at your values can give you key insights into why you do what you do and how you make decisions. If you don't like your values, then you have an opportunity to do some personal change work. Perhaps you decided early in life that you can't have both money and love. Maybe your need for freedom from family members is really a protection against needy people. Our values are what fuel our passion, what motivate us, and what we love. Eliciting your own values is an excellent way to take stock and see what is really driving your behavior.

Treasure Hunt

Early memories help form your values. Reactivate the kite strings of your early happy memories and reminisce about how those memories helped form your positive attributes as an adult. Remember the support, the love, the companionship, the camaraderie, and the friendship you experienced. How did these things provide a strong foundation for your character today? Looking at the early events that helped form your character and your values, write down the things you value today that are rooted in those early experiences. They are valuable resources to support you through difficult times.

Take stock of where you are, and compare it to where you want to be. Here are some examples: (1) Currently I'm working for someone else, but what I really want is to own my own company. (2) I'm a cashier at a restaurant, but my dream is to become a well paid chef. (3) I'm living with pleasant roommates, but I really long for a relationship and a home of my own.

When you chose to elicit your values in a certain area of your life, it probably is an area with which you are not completely happy. Or perhaps you want to experience better results, more satisfaction, or some sort of change. Think about what you currently have versus what you would like to have. You may want to draw a line down the center of a page and list the present conditions and results on one side with the desired conditions and results on the other.

Next, review the differences between what currently is and what you desire. There is great value in holding the tension between these two things. Hold them both in your mind at the same time, letting your thoughts free-flow for a while. Try not to jump to any solutions or plans of action too quickly. The key is to experience the differences between what is and what can be. The longer you hold the tension between the two, the higher the ultimate resolution is likely to be.

Look at an area of your life through the prism of your values. Now refer to the top three on the list of values you created earlier. In the area you're dealing with, they are what drive your behavior. Can you see how they are reflected in your current situation? Now take a look at what you desire and how your top three values support it. Will your top three values, as prime motivators of your behavior and your results, get you where you want to be? If not, this is an area for you to do some change work.

Identify your top values in several more areas of your life. This values work will be used later.

Chapter 19

Balancing Acts

You can do anything but not everything.[93]

—David Allen

When I chose to spend a year deepening my understanding of balance, my life suddenly became filled with extremes that demanded balance. As the midway point between potential extremes, like dancing on the edge of a sword, balance requires constant microadjustments to maintain. I immersed myself in play, that joie de vivre that brings a healthy balance to intense work. At the same time I began major work projects that demanded new levels of creativity and skill. Work was my passion and motivation, while play provided camaraderie, rest, and fitness as an antidote to burnout. By passionately committing to both work and play, I soon became excruciatingly aware that something had to give!

Do What You Love

I first prioritized what was most important to me (see the Treasure Hunt in the previous chapter) to identify those things that gave me juice and love, that I would choose above others. For me, it was a combination of work and play, and with that in mind, I committed to revitalizing what I spent energy on. Like squeezing a wet sponge, I eliminated the less important things. Just saying no became easier because I had committed to doing what was most vital to me. I had created a template for choosing how to spend my time. If you love your family but spend all your time at work, in the long run you could say you really don't value family. We vote with our time about what we value, and that requires ruthless balance.

Clara grew up in an international commune. Mostly separated from her parents, she was raised in a collective, strict, controlling environment. A long history of abuse, a domineering husband, five children, and religious dicta molded her into a compliant, submissive, and depressed woman. Her only outlet was dance, which she had learned in China, India, and college. And dance she did! It was the only self-expression she was allowed, and she danced her emotions and pain with intensity. Eventually she left the marriage, with no means of support for her children. She reunited with her parents to begin healing their relationship. She also started healing herself through creating her story in dance, a series of powerful vignettes accompanied by her recorded voice weaving the tales with the music and movement. She danced the submissive feminine, surrendering to authority and living entirely for others, until she uncovered the deep well of *self* inside, her source of inner strength and power. Only then was she able to feel compassion, love, and forgiveness. Only then was she able to care for her children. She danced the healing balance, which spoke to the core in all of us, finding our demons and shadow sides to reconcile them with our purposeful parts.

Start, Stop, Maintain or Change

- Start: You need new clothes to fit changing times, images, and activities.
- Stop: If you never threw away any of your clothes, your closet would be a hopeless jumble of useful and no-longer-useful items.
- Maintain or change: Clothes require regular cleaning and fixing. Outworn items have to be replaced.

We are habitually better at some of these things than others. Ask yourself which activities—start, stop, maintain or change—you do best and which you do worst. Do you find it easy or hard to generate new ideas and projects? Can you keep things running by fixing or changing, or does maintenance bore you? Do you complete things or let them drag on and on? Do you ruthlessly toss outmoded or unused stuff? Once you have taken realistic stock of your tendencies, it is time to bring more balance in these areas. Flow in life depends on balancing these three. On a spreadsheet, answer these questions:

- What am I not starting that I need to?
- What can I start?
- What am I not maintaining or changing that I could?
- What needs more maintenance or care?
- What am I not completing that I need to?
- What can I stop doing?

Law of Three—Tension between Opposites Creates Movement
Consider a couple dancing together; each must maintain a certain amount of tension while simultaneously being attentive to the other in order to create the dance. If either partner collapses or tries to dominate, it is no longer a dance. The dance occurs because of the balance between the two.

There is a maxim that nothing new is ever created without opposites. Whether it is male–female, freedom–structure, or current situation–desired outcome, all creativity demands two opposing forces in order to birth, invent, or accomplish a third, new element. Once you understand this principle of using the tension between opposing forces, you can consciously apply it to moving forward in your life.

Ana loves the freedom to choose in the moment what to do and to follow her intuition. She wants to be a writer, and she has set aside several hours each day to write. Even though she finds this daily grind very confining, she is using the tension between confinement and her natural desire for spontaneity to elevate her writing skills and achieve her goal. Picture a climber who wants to go up a steep crevice with no toeholds on it. The smart climber will put his back to one wall and feet against the opposite wall, using the tension between the two to "shinny up" (a Southern technical term) to the top.

Just Say No

Do you ever find yourself getting pulled into something because you don't want to hurt someone's feelings, you want to be nice, you want to gain approval, or you'll feel guilty if you don't? A friend's email was totally shut down because someone had sent her a file that used up all her computer memory with photos. Once that file was removed and the memory freed, she could receive her emails again. This is a great metaphor for how we let relatively unimportant things in life clog up the flow. Fighting monotony means taking habitual things off automatic so that we will have the time to do what feeds our passion, joy, and satisfaction.

Oranges and Raisins

Balancing your time requires first knowing what you want to accomplish and then separating big projects into smaller tasks that let you use time efficiently. If you fill a bowl with oranges, there is still room for pecans. Then you can put in raisins. When that's full, you can still pour sugar into the bowl. And then there's room for water. By dividing a large project (filling a bowl) into large tasks (oranges) and smaller tasks (pecans, raisins, and so on), you can fit them into little bits of otherwise wasted time. Looming projects can be less daunting, getting started can be easier, and procrastination will be less likely when you can break the tasks down into smaller chunks. Whenever you really, really want to do something, you will find the time to fit it in. Time is elastic like that.

Principles for Balance

Consider these principles to create balance in your life:

- Choose Your Passions
  Consciously decide what you value most, what you love deeply and most want to accomplish, and spend your time there.

- Closet Cleaning
  Use the start, stop, maintain or change model to find and fix what is out of balance.

- Law of Three
  Balance and forward movement are accomplished by becoming conscious about the opposing forces involved, including the emotional ones, and then reconciling them.

- Just Say No
  It takes ruthless courage to stick with what you value rather than succumb to less important requests. But if you don't, you may overload your system or end up with something less than what you truly value.

- Oranges and Raisins
  Break large projects down into tasks that can be fit into smaller chunks of time that might otherwise be wasted.

Treasure Hunt
Decide which of the three, Start, Stop, or Maintain, you are best at, second best at, and worst at:

Best: _____
Second best: _____
Third best: _____

Now, find the places where your life is out of balance. Where do you not have enough time? Where do different areas of your life compete for your attention? Use the suggested spreadsheet questions above for the areas out of balance. Then apply the principles for balance to complete a plan for ruthless action. All that is left is to put your crafted plan into action!

Chapter 20

Let's Get Physical—
Does the Body-Mind Mind?

> There is more wisdom in your body than in your deepest philosophy.[94]
>
> —Friedrich Nietzsche

Is there a connection between the physical body and the mind? Imagine you are holding a large ripe lemon. You scratch the peel and sniff that lemony smell. Now imagine you cut it in half and sniff the inside. Lick it. By now you are probably experiencing something in your mouth, like a puckering or salivating, and maybe your face is changing a bit. Too often people scoff at the effects of holistic remedies such as acupuncture, prayer, or Reiki, saying, "That's all in your mind." Or maybe you think a medicine or homeopathic you take is just a placebo. "It's just a placebo" implies that what you are taking doesn't work because it's all in your head. The fact is that placebos work 40 percent of the time—a better record than many medicines. How does a placebo work so effectively?

Until 1986, there was no scientific proof of the mind-body connection. Throughout history mystics and regular people have believed that thoughts could influence reality or at least the body, but there was no scientific proof. Then, neuroscientist Dr. Candace Pert, working with neurotransmitters, discovered the connection. In her fascinating, novel-like book, *Molecules of Emotion*, she describes her pioneering research on how the chemicals inside our bodies form a dynamic information network, linking brain and body.

Her revolutionary work explains how emotional states or moods are produced by the body's neuropeptides and the scientific basis for the popular wisdom about having gut feelings. What we experience as an emotion is produced by the activation of a particular neuronal circuit simultaneously throughout the brain and the body. Since neurotransmitters and their receptors are in both the brain and the rest of body, the mind is in the body as well as the brain. Deepak Chopra popularized this by saying "Every cell in your body is eavesdropping on your thoughts."[95]

This discovery of the body-mind connection could be as revolutionary as discovering the earth is round. If we adjust our thinking accordingly, the changes can affect all aspects of our lives. In education, for example, school programs that involve the entire body in the learning process through art, dance, singing, and movement seem to be more successful, particularly with hyperactive children. ADD-diagnosed children cease being a problem in a learning environment that engages all their body-mind senses.

> Somewhere in the vast treasure trove of the body/mind, I am convinced, we remember everything we have learnt over the past fifteen billion years. We are the ultimate evolutionary hybrids, and the vigor of human genetic inheritance, if we could but claim it and work with it, it is more than enough for us to get on with it.[96]
>
> —Jean Houston

Emotional health provides another example. Unresolved negative emotions are stored in the neurology of the body. Two ways to clear them are through bodywork and mental/emotional therapy, with a combination of the two often recommended. A frustrated, angry person might find peace of mind by working out, running, massage, or yoga. A backache might have an emotional basis, such as a fear of not being supported, which, when emotionally cleared, allows the physical backache to vanish. A client was in the hospital for bleeding ulcers. In a Time Dimension Therapy session, his experience of the ulcers as a big band across his abdomen led to a past-life recall, which he reframed, bringing the new experience back to his present life. Immediately afterward, the hospital's test revealed that the ulcers had completely disappeared.

In the area of spirituality, you can't achieve a prayerful, meditative state through the intellect. You can enter the trancelike state from which to slip into deep meditation by first engaging the body in activities like chanting, singing, yoga, and breathing. Many find keeping their body fit, as their temple, through good nutrition, exercise, balance, and quality time with loved ones, allows them to experience their spirituality more deeply.

Treasure Hunt

As food for thought, consider your own body-mind connections for a week. If you have any body discomfort, look at your thoughts to see if there is a link. Physical behaviors and symptoms are often metaphors. Jaw clenching, for example, can be related to something held in and not expressed, diabetes to lack of sweetness in life, shoulders to shouldering too many burdens or other peoples' burdens, back pain to lack of support, and knee pain to blocking forward movement.[97] If you are dealing with emotional issues, complement your work by adding physical releases such as bodywork, acupuncture, yoga, and exercise. If you are learning something new, engage all body senses in the process rather than just your brain. If you want to deepen your spiritual practice, it is said that you must descend fully into the physical before you can ascend to the spiritual. This process allows you to become more conscious of where you deny and where you fully rely on your body-mind connection in your daily life.

Chapter 21

Body Wisdom

> Our inner guidance comes to us through our feelings and body wisdom first—not through intellectual understanding.[98]
>
> —Christiane Northrup

Beyond Conscious Awareness

To pass the time in a long grocery line, my daughter and I experimented with a can of regular Coke and a can of Diet Coke. Without peeking to see which it was, she held one and then the other as I muscle-tested her. She was always weaker with the sugared one—but how could her body detect which had sugar? Soon the entire grocery line was engrossed in our experiment!

There are many noninvasive techniques for tapping into the body's wisdom to identify ailments and nutritional and emotional needs. Try some of them! Your body can pick up energies that you consciously have no clue about. Here are three methods you may enjoy experimenting with.

Muscle testing (known as applied kinesiology) engages the subconscious mind to initiate physical responses to such yes–no questions as "Should I take a vitamin D supplement?" or "Am I allergic to garlic?" or even "Did I know him in a past life?" In the form of muscle testing known as the arm test, the subject holds her arm out parallel to the floor. The tester asks (or thinks) the question and pushes down lightly on the arm. If the arm remains strong and parallel, the answers is yes. With a no answer, the arm can't help dropping.

A related method is the sway test. The subject holds the object being tested in her hand or against her diaphragm and asks the question. (If no object is involved, just ask the question.) A forward sway usually indicates yes, and a backward sway means no.

Many people trust a pendulum, which can be a crystal or other lightly weighted object dangling from a string or chain. Holding the chain lightly with two fingers, ask the question. The subconscious mind will initiate tiny movements, causing your hand to set the pendulum swinging.

With each technique, it's essential to calibrate by asking a series of questions to which you know the answers so as to learn your personal signals for yes and no. Or simply ask, "Please show me a yes. Please show me a no."

Love attractions work in a similar mysterious way—pheromones, smell, some inner Geiger counter or sensing radar that attracts you to one and repels you from another. Ever been in a crowd where you want to avoid someone merely because of their vibe? Or on the freeway have you felt compelled to move away from a nearby car for no apparent reason? Just yesterday I followed my feelings and avoided an accident by moving away from a car, only to have it sideswipe the truck behind me. Frequently when I put my hands on a massage client to connect with them, they exclaim that I'm touching the exact spot where their trouble is! On those occasions, I have to admit that my head has no clue—it's all body wisdom; I'm allowing the body to do its thing.

Body Wisdom Potential

We have ten to the tenth to the eleventh power of potential neurological connections in our body, several hundred gazillion, if we're counting.[99] Yet we use a mere 5 to 10 percent of our mental and physical capacities.

We are structured holographically, with every part containing the blueprint for the whole. Most of our senses can be replicated by other senses. Blind people, for example, can separate red yarn from blue by "seeing" with their touch.[100]

Skin is our major sense organ. We breathe through our skin. It's not like Saran Wrap, even though it keeps out bacteria and foreign substances. It can absorb or repel.

And it is amazing what unconscious powers we have over our bodies. Under hypnosis, a client was able to anesthetize a part of his body by making it cold and unmovable. There was a time when a nurse wasn't able to give me a shot because somehow my body tightened the blood vessel, causing the needle to slide off. It took a good twenty minutes for my conscious mind to persuade my unconscious mind to override my body's resistance.

A teacher of mine was totally deaf, yet once she met a person, she was able to talk to them, even by phone, by tuning in with some other sense. Once I tested her ability by mentally asking her a question as she was walking away from me. I thought, *What restaurant are we going to?* The hair on my body stood up and my mouth dropped when she turned around and answered me! She later explained she was able to hear with other senses, including visualizing and kinesthetic vibrations.

Mind-Body Connection

Every day of his life, a client of mine woke up with a backache. Medical checks revealed no physical cause. Through a guided visualization, he went back in time to age five, the first time he'd felt resentment, and remembered his mother got sick and couldn't play with him anymore. That was when he decided that he'd have to stiffen up and do it all himself. After he persuaded that little five-year-old to make a different decision that gave him more choice and flexibility, he never had a backache again.

In 1986 Dr. Candace Pert discovered that the mind and body are intricately connected, like heads and tails of a coin, via the neurotransmitters. Our emotions are not just *controlled by* our hormones and peptides; they *are* our chemical neurotransmitters.

What we feel as an emotion is literally a chemical that our body produces.

One way to influence our emotions is by how we view the world. When we change our internal representations of the world, the pictures, sounds, and feelings we store as memories, we can change who we are. When we change our mind, we change our body by the instant communication between mind and body via the neurotransmitters. That's how the woman with multiple personalities could have diabetes with one personality, and it would instantly disappear when she changed to the other. Because the second personality didn't have the same life experiences, values, and memories that the first one did, it didn't have diabetes. Now how could the change happen instantly? It is because the only way we know how to be who we are is by our memories, our values and beliefs, and the stories we tell ourselves. When those are changed, we instantly morph into someone who fits the new version.

Listening to Your Body Wisdom
Listening to the body takes trust and attention to its subtle signals. It takes learning to make finer and finer sensory distinctions. It is easy to think you are imagining your body's messages or to override them with head logic. The more we listen, the more the body is encouraged to share its wisdom. Like all of us, it loves to be listened to!

Treasure Hunt
You may want to explore your body's wisdom outside of your conscious awareness. You can try muscle testing, for example, the sway technique, or some other method you may have learned or devised to connect with your physical body. To establish a baseline, test foods that are known to be good for you and foods known to be bad. Then test foods about which you are unsure. You may be surprised to find that your body can't tolerate some foods generally thought to be good. Some don't tolerate onions and garlic, while others don't do well with grains such as wheat, corn, barley, and rye,

and still others can't eat a high-meat diet. Test your response to soy, milk, chocolate, wheat, corn, and spices like cinnamon.

You can extend beyond foods to include your body's responses to medications and supplements. You can identify which people and environments are beneficial to you and which are not. You can ask about a location for your new office or home, for example. As you pay attention to your body's subtle messages, notice how accurate your testing becomes.

Section V

Shifting Perspectives to Enhance Changes

In section IV you practiced inner change work on the following:

- transforming and updating your beliefs
- aligning your words, your thoughts, and your beliefs
- finding the values that determine your focus, your results, and your evaluation of how you did
- creating balance and alignment in your life
- exploring your body-mind connections
- listening to your body wisdom

> Looking at problems from different angles actually lessens the mental burden.[101]
>
> —Dalai Lama

In section V you will continue to change within as you explore different perspectives to shift the prism through which you view your life.

- Often it takes different points of view of a problem to get unstuck from a recurring, limiting pattern or unproductive emotion.
- We are energetic beings rather than merely bodies with parts. Going beyond the edge of what is normally considered possible, what I call the nth factor, is a way to harness your energetic potentials and faculties to enhance your well-being.
- Opening to the grace of receiving creates a loving flow between give and take, making your heart available to love, connection, and greater spirituality.
- Exploring past lives as a way to resolve an issue or shift your point of view can give you new metaphors to expand your potential.
- Connection with your ancestors, remembered or imagined from a distant past, can give you a sense of connection and belonging to a greater whole, as well as provide valuable support and resources.

By now you've experienced how the Treasure Hunts guide your inner explorations, so it's time for you to design your own, to take your change work in the direction you desire to fit your situation and needs. Individualized questions, food for thought, and optional directions will be provided to stimulate your creations. Remember, the premise of this book is that we have the answers within ourselves.

Chapter 22

How to Coax Your Inner-Truth Cat to Sit on Your Lap

I am always doing that which I can not do, in order that
I may learn how to do it.[102]

—Vincent van Gogh

Have you ever tried to herd cats or force a cat to sit or stay on your lap? Coaxing the Muse of Inner Truth to visit you is a little like that. When I was working in a corporate management job (another lifetime), management was having difficulties resolving issues with the union. New approaches were desperately needed to reduce the mounting tensions. During a weekend in a cabin near Mount Ashland, I emptied my mind and asked for a new solution. Every time I started talking to myself or ruminating over the current stressful events (called "obsessively worrying"), I stopped and reissued the desire for a new solution. I reemptied my mind and waited. After what seemed a very long time, I saw my two hands, one clenched in a fist and the other open. That simple image became the template for working out an agreement—stand firm on bottom-line issues, and extend an open-handed, flexible approach to others. In itself it wasn't a solution, but it was an effective means of designing an approach that worked.

Like a sweet spring, a child's ability to imagine and play make-believe is constantly flowing. As adults, we can reclaim this same ease of visualizing when we just make it up. There is nothing to have performance anxiety about, because there is no right or wrong answer. Finding a solution to a problem or achieving release from a nagging negative emotion or destructive pattern is finding our inner truth. Inner truths come when we open ourselves up and let ideas flow into us. We've all spent time worrying obsessively over a problem, going over and over the same thoughts, escalating our anxiety and bad feelings. That slams the door to the Inner-Truth Muse! We do this loopy worrying in our heads. To invite the muse, we need to move into our hearts and our bodies.

With our left-brain intellect, we figure things out—from concepts, principles, and design to flowcharts, timetables, and evaluations. Sometimes, however, we get stuck in a problem, an unproductive emotion, or a recurring limiting pattern, and despite all logic to the contrary, we keep repeating it! Intellectually we can see that our behavior is unproductive or self-destructive, but we can't seem to break out of it. This is when we can invite our Muse of Inner Truth to inspire us or our Inner-Truth Cat to come and sit on our lap.

Like wiggling a nail back and forth to free it from a hole, the idea is to keep looking at the problem pattern from different perspectives. Often it takes more than one perspective for it to finally come loose. Here are five perspectives that can help:

Time Perspective

How long has the problem existed? Go back to before you had that pattern and notice how it feels, your opinion of yourself, and your view of life when you didn't have the problem. What caused you to create the problem? How did you rationalize it? What alternatives would be more useful to you? Now go out into the future to a point where you no longer have this problem. Notice how it feels and what you learned in order to let go of the pattern. How far out into the future did you have to go—a year, five years, or even twenty years? What finally resolved the issue? This exercise may not lift or erase the problem, but it may ease it. You are just wiggling the nail back and forth to extract it from the hole.

View from Outside Self

When we scrutinize the problem from outside ourselves, we frequently get fresh ideas. Look at your problem as if you were someone else, like your partner or a respected mentor. How would that person see you? What would they see that you couldn't see while you were stuck in it? Now rise above your life and look down on the whole situation. Go high enough to distance yourself from the emotions. From this dissociated perspective, seeing the big picture, what insights do you gain?

Place of Planning (POP)

Go to a time before you were conceived, to the Place of Planning, where you made decisions about coming into this life. You'll make this up out of your imagination. A POP takes you to where you were before you came into existence, moving you out of your current situation. It implies there is an overarching plan for your life. It can be a place where you (re)connect with the Divine, guides, wise beings, or your higher self and other resources. It can provide a refuge where you can ask questions, get direction and information, and reset your coming life. How you imagine your own unique POP and what you use it for can be a rich resource for you. Notice how it feels there. What differences do you notice between this and your present situation? What sources of love and support do you find in your Place of Planning? You may discover a book or a receptacle of knowledge there as well. Open it and read your three purposes for this life. Reconnect with them and bring them with you back to the present. Now that you remember your real purpose for being here, what has shifted?

Before It Existed

The emotion or problem didn't always exist. Go back in time, even if you have to go to a past life or before you came into being. Make it up. Go back, back, back until you arrive at a place *before* you were caught in the problem trance. What is different about your perspective? How do you feel about yourself? How has your self-esteem shifted?

Once you get to a period before the emotional problem existed, you have moved yourself beyond the trance, and all you need to do now is pay attention to things you couldn't see when you were in it.

Reframe

What point of view can you adopt that will alter the way you experience the problem? My cat was getting old and had developed some obnoxious habits, like yowling loudly in the corner so he could hear himself because he was going deaf, and staying outside and only coming in to poop on the floor. I was becoming quite upset with him. Then I reframed the situation—I told myself he might not be around much longer, so I should enjoy him while I could. Every time he yowled, I cuddled and loved him, remembering to enjoy every minute he was still alive. Not only did I become calmer, but also he behaved better. Not doing well at something? Oh, that just means you are learning! Your children don't call you as much as you'd like? How wonderful that you raised them so well that they don't need to constantly ask for advice and money. (Well, that one may be admittedly a bit far-fetched.)

Whichever methods you choose, put yourself in a daydreamy, meditative trance in some quiet, relaxed place, and invite your sweet Inner-Truth Cat to play. You are opening yourself up to a vast wealth of multidimensional richness, there for the asking when you allow your mind to empty and make it up.

Treasure Hunt

Now is the time for you to devise a Treasure Hunt that will take you even deeper into your personal change work.

Time Perspective

The pattern was created at some point, so there must be a time before it existed. You might devise a unique way to go before that point. One day the friend with whom I was playing tennis complained that she had lost her confidence and couldn't seem to hit the ball well. I suggested that she imagine she could somersault backward up in the air and land in her past. She alighted in her childhood, when she was happy, confident, and playful. I suggested that she bring those good feelings back to the present as a resource on the tennis court. When we resumed playing, she beat me! The idea of flipping backward that I made up to get her out of her funk worked—too well!

View from Outside Self
There are several viewpoints you can play with, as follows:

- as you see the situation
- as someone else sees it
- as someone else sees you and what they think of how you see it
- from above looking down on the total scene, larger than both you and the other person's views, incorporating all possibilities. Instead of taking a particular perspective, you are viewing the whole and all possible viewpoints.

Place of Planning (POP)
As you imagine the POP, you will discover your three purposes for coming into existence. You may envision the source of this information as a book, a scroll, a light, a fire, a chalice, or a wise being. It is your mind, so take whatever comes to mind. With this knowledge you can reclaim your sense of your life's purpose.

Existence implies duality. If you came into this life with the very powerful purpose of love, for example, chances are you have experienced the opposite of love. In order to truly express love, you will have to know its opposite—every coin has two sides. Since you've already experienced lack of love, you've done the hard part. From the POP where you recaptured your life's true purpose, you can bring this knowledge back with you as you reenter existence; now you can enjoy full expression of the love that is your true purpose!

Before It Existed
You are continuing to develop and hone your skills at moving back and forth in time, at envisioning, and at noticing your changes of state as you do so. You are becoming friends with your unconscious mind and the unique way it works.

Reframe
Reframing a situation takes a lot of practice. To learn to reframe, I used to practice taking negative statements to see if I could shift the speaker's perspective or attitude. Some reframes didn't work or were a bit off-putting, so I'd try another and another until I could see their negativity diminish. Here are examples of what I said (some more successful or less obnoxious than others!):

"I feel so bad with this cold!"

- It's a good excuse to get some needed rest.
- At least you're alive to have only a cold.
- That means your body is building an immunity to the flu or worse.

"Bad drivers make me so angry!"

- At least you're a good enough driver to notice bad ones and not to make other people angry with your good driving.
- Since there are a lot of bad drivers on the road, you won't have to worry about falling asleep at the wheel!
- That makes you a good defensive driver and keeps you safe.

"I hate it when people criticize me."

- They're just jealous.
- It probably means they feel critical of themselves. It says a lot more about them than you, don't you think?

- They just want the best for you and are probably trying to be helpful.
- It's a good thing you don't always accept other people's viewpoints as valid!
- What would the world be like if no one ever expressed a different point of view?

Chapter 23

The Nth Factor

> Built into you is an internal guidance system that shows
> you the way home. All you need to do is heed the voice.[103]
> —Neale Donald Walsch

Why do some people quickly get over the flu or never miss a day of work while others are down for weeks? Obviously many factors enter into this: good nutrition, rest, exercise, a loving support system, spirituality, and a positive attitude, not to mention good genes and sometimes plain old luck. There may be something else that comes into play, which I've named the nth factor, something far less tangible and possibly more important to our energetic well-being.

I define the nth factor as the ability to move beyond the exterior world to tap an inner resource. It may be drawn from our mind-body's ability to tap into a greater source of energy. Whether we call it God, deep implicate-order intelligence, or a quantum energy field, it is a vast well of potential.

People often respond to treatments that appear unscientific. With the placebo effect, for example, people react to sugar pills the same as to medicine a whopping 40 percent of the time. Such spiritual practices as prayer, revivals, and Reiki all have documented successes. Thousands of instances have been recorded of people with terminal diseases having spontaneous remissions, and of tumors and illnesses disappearing for unexplained reasons.

There is growing evidence that we are energetic beings rather than bodies with parts that work mechanically the way a car does. A brief review of some of these areas will get us on the same page:

Quantum Physics

Replacing the mechanistic Newtonian physics, quantum physics has discovered that at the lowest subatomic level of matter, we are highly oscillating bits of virtual energy. We are mostly space with an electromagnetic force field that makes us appear solid. Subatomic particles can move backward and forward in time.[104] If you turn one of twin particles separated in space, the other will turn at the same time. I experienced this looking at a sample of my blood in a dark-field scope. When I became upset, my blood sample reacted by becoming very agitated, even though it was outside of my body ("Made my blood boil!"). Recent research with CERN's Large Hadron Collider has discovered a tiny virtual reality particle that winks in and out of existence, going back and forth between a particle and energy. Called the Higgs boson and sometimes the "God particle," it supposedly holds the electrons of the atoms in their orbits, keeping them from collapsing.[105] These tiny virtual particles form a soup that bathes us all, connecting us.

Mind-Body Connection via Neurotransmitters

In 1986 Dr. Candace Pert's groundbreaking research[106] provided scientific proof that the mind and body function together as an integrated system and that our emotions are chemicals. Emotions are linked to physical pain, as proven by John E. Sarno, MD.[107] He asserts that back pain is only rarely the result of structural problems; rather, it stems from muscular tension of repressed emotional problems. The simple act of acknowledging the emotional component has caused many of Dr. Sarno's patients' back pain to disappear.

Auras and Energetic Fields around Living Things

Dr. Valerie Hunt developed a scientific means of videotaping the human aura.[108] In one instance, she showed a woman's aura grow large and white as she moved into deep meditation. When her young son ran in front of her, her aura bent toward him and turned pink. Kirlian photography[109] has captured the energy patterns coming off living things, such as the energetic difference between a hand at rest and one giving Reiki, and the higher life force of organic as opposed to regular foods.

Our Holographic Nature

When something is holographic, it means that every part contains the blueprint of the whole. When you shine a laser beam through a holographic plate, you get a 3-D image, like R2-D2's images in *Star Wars*. If you were to tear that plate into tiny pieces and shine a laser light through any piece, you would get the same 3-D image! Studies with salamanders (which remain alive although in a stupor when their brains are removed) showed that when the scientist minced up a brain and reinserted even a few cells, the salamander could still function.[110] A respected mathematician with an IQ of 120 was found in an autopsy only to have a few brain cells around the perimeter of his neocortex. He had recreated (holographically?) his normal brain functions from these few cells. Such distinguished scientists as David Bohm, Karl Pribram, Ilya Prigogine, and Rupert Sheldrake have produced studies of the holographic nature of the universe.

New Order or Chaos?

Why, you may ask, should we care about this nth factor? In a world that is growing more complex and overburdened with information, we'll arrive at a breaking point where we either evolve to a new way of being or succumb to the chaos of overload. We need more efficient ways to cope. (If all telephone calls still required a human operator to manually connect them, we'd need to employ well over half the population in the United States to do it.) It is in this arena where the nth factor comes to the fore.

How Can You Develop Your Nth Factor?

Here are some suggestions:

- Be aware of your thoughts and beliefs. If you think your immune system is strong, it probably is. If you think you'll get the flu, you probably will. Take inventory of your subliminal programmings to see if they reflect what you want. If they don't, what do you have to do to shift your habitual beliefs?

- Be aware of what is energetically good and what is energetically toxic for you. Work to eliminate things that energetically weaken you. Causes can include being around a certain person, watching a violent TV program or the news, or even listening to gossip. Fill your life with those things that give your energy a boost or act as a balm—good music, walk in nature, meditation, the company of loving friends.

- Take the time to tap into your inner resources. In *Jump Time*, Jean Houston urges us to take an hour every morning while the external world is still quiet to journey, meditate, and download energy and information. Whether you prefer journaling, spiritual practice, having a chat with your higher self, choose your personal way.

- How will you strengthen your nth factor to stimulate your energetic well-being and expand time to soothe your resource-stretched life?

Treasure Hunt

You may want to write about times you have recovered from or reversed an illness or injury, taking special care to describe the resources you called upon in the process. As you make this list, you are in a sense fortifying your belief that you actually have an nth factor ability.

What are your personal beliefs about your ability to be healthy, your ability to recover from injury or illness, and your emotional and physical strengths? My husband, for example, believes he heals very quickly, and so he does.

What higher powers and resources do you call on in times of need? What do you do for relaxation and happiness? This may include nurturing friendships, being with family, caring for a pet, or engaging in a passionate hobby such as gardening. Many years ago, my sister was diagnosed with stage IV ovarian cancer. She was open to all forms of treatment, including chemotherapy and surgery, as well as prayer. I searched for any prayer groups that would include her, and by the time she was in complete remission, twenty-six groups were praying for her! It's twelve years later and she's still very healthy.

What ways can you devise to strengthen your personal nth factor? What results do you get when you use these?

Chapter 24

The Grace of Receiving:
What's Spiritual about Receiving?

Thousands of candles can be lighted from a single candle, and the life of the candle will not be shortened. Happiness is never decreased by being shared.[111]

—Buddha

How many times has someone wanted to give you something and, even though you could use it, you refused? A dear friend wanted to buy me a beautiful watch with crushed opals in the face, but I just couldn't let him do it. Your guest says, "Let me help you clean up." "That's okay," you say, beginning to (over)explain. "I know where everything goes, and it'll be easier just to do it myself." Or a friend offers you a lift. "No," you reply, "I already bought my bus ticket, so I'd better use it!"

Often we refuse help, gifts, and even companionship from dear friends and family. There's something about accepting that's hard. The question is, how can we believe it's spiritual to receive when we've been taught that it is better to give than to receive?

What might motivate this resistance to receiving? Do you believe that a little receiving is good but that too much receiving is selfish? Are you afraid that you might be indebted to the giver, dependent on them in some way? In this give-and-take accounting, now you would owe them a favor, and rather than be obligated, it might be easier not to accept their offer. Besides, some people use giving as a means of manipulation, a way to buy your love or to weasel in to get something for themselves, so it's just safer not to receive.

It could be a trust issue: If you open yourself up to receiving from someone, you could get burned. Or they could betray you or let you down. Perhaps it is better not to let anyone in. It is certainly safer than being vulnerable to heartache. "My son relies on me," you might tell yourself. "If I rely on someone else and they betray me, then I'm putting my son at risk." Or maybe you say, "I don't need anyone to help me. I can do this myself." "If I don't receive from you, you won't get close to me and you can't hurt me."

Underneath, perhaps you feel a deep sense of unworthiness. One of the most common problems holding us back from achieving our full potential is a nagging (or full-blown!) sense of inadequacy, a lack of self-worth, and guilt or shame. Frequently, children take on the responsibility and guilt for everything around them, including divorce, abandonment, abuse, and molestation. They decide that somehow they weren't good enough, because if they were, the negative thing wouldn't have happened. This could turn into becoming a people pleaser: "I felt so unworthy as a kid that when I would babysit, if the parents offered me a glass of juice or a cookie, I couldn't even accept because of a deep, gnawing feeling of being unworthy."

If the above didn't light up your circuits about receiving, perhaps you are selfish and think the world owes you a living! Or maybe you are well-balanced with a healthy sense of self-worth, trust, and security, and appropriate boundaries. The discussion so far isn't so much about reasons why it is not okay to receive as it is about recognizing our relationship to receiving as indicators or signals for an opportunity for personal growth, for ferreting out our own issues of trust, safety, betrayal, self-worth, guilt, and shame. I once asked a client who found receiving impossible to open up to receive the warmth of the sun. He couldn't even accept that until he cleared issues with his own self-worth!

Suppose the many times we shut ourselves off from receiving actually block our spirituality. To open your heart to God, to spirituality, and even to love and connectedness requires receiving in the highest sense. Accepting something (that you feel is appropriate to accept) can be turned into a spiritual practice. For example, the next time someone compliments you, allow that to feed your self-worthiness, opening your heart to the grace of receiving. Receiving may be the highest form of connectedness and spirituality!

You can build up a tolerance to receiving without feeling guilty. While writing this section, I practiced receiving and noticed my own reactions. Friends appeared from every corner to push my "receiving" buttons with compliments and helpful gestures. Sometimes I was able to gracefully receive, and sometimes I resisted, thought of ways to pay them back, or felt undeserving. I hadn't been aware of how many times I shunned receiving. It got better: Yesterday I sneezed in Home Depot, and two separate people immediately said, "God bless you!" I smiled at the grace.

Treasure Hunt

Each person has their own attitude toward receiving. Start by taking an inventory of your abilities to receive—whom you receive from, whom you gracefully receive from, and whom you find it difficult to receive from. What can you receive gracefully, and what makes you uncomfortable or causes you to feel a need to even the score? Where do you expect to receive? Who gives you the most? What is your relationship between gratefulness and receiving?

Perhaps you will design a series of questions to help you uncover deeper issues whenever receiving makes you uncomfortable.

A daily practice of being grateful for what you have received can align you with your spiritual connection. Some keep gratitude lists—a friend makes beautiful notebooks for people to write ten things they are grateful for every day. Others, as they go to bed, name the reasons for gratitude that the day has brought them.

Examine the flow of giving and receiving in your life to see if either is out of alignment. What can you do to restore balance?

Chapter 25

Up for Grabs

Have you ever considered past-life regression or therapy, either out of curiosity or to resolve some issues? Our society puts great emphasis on left-brain, analytical, rational thinking. To balance this, we can practice more right-brain, intuitive processing. One way is to explore possible past lives. It is up for grabs whether this produces nothing more than a daydream fantasy or results in an expanded consciousness of self-reinvention.

High in the Peruvian Andes our little group excitedly followed our leader, Kevin Ryerson, to the entrance to Machu Picchu. As we entered the ancient grounds, I began to feel lethargic. This was unusual since we had acclimatized for a week at a higher elevation. Soon, I could hardly walk; I felt as if I weighed a ton. When I asked Kevin, he said it was probably sadness. Without warning tears began rolling down my cheeks. I sobbed all the way through our tour, puzzled by where such a flood of emotions could be coming from.

At the top of the ruins lay a sundial, where a group member did a past-life reading for me. He said that I had been left there by my beloved father, who went away to fight the Spanish, and I never saw him again. In the ensuing days of our visit, I scrambled like a mountain goat over the steep terraces, even climbing the daunting Huayna Picchu peak with ease. My Spanish became more fluent as if I were truly at home. Memories? Perhaps. But when I first visited Machu Picchu with my family at age fifteen, I felt the same lethargic sadness, the same struggle to move! Recently, I returned again to Machu Picchu. This time, however, the feelings the place had stirred in me were absent. The hordes of tourists walking the set path around its perimeter obliterated my sense of connection with the place. At the end of the day, after most of the tourists had departed, I slipped into the room with the Birthing Stone, a large slab where women gave birth. When I snapped a photo, I thought my camera was broken because of the streak of light across the image. But it was the sun's rays from the peak of Huayna Picchu falling directly on the Birthing Stone. I like to think it was Machu Picchu recognizing me and saying hello. At the time, I was hard at work on this book, and Machu Picchu seemed to be encouraging me to carry on and give it birth. (See photo under Part Two, Three Simple Guidelines, Guideline 1: Life Is a Point of View.)

Some people, particularly children, have a strong knowing about a former life. I once talked to a preschooler who insisted that he was a famous soccer player "before." He was quite matter-of-fact about it, supplying many details. Other times, as it was for me in Machu Picchu, the memories are like swirling, shadowy dream stuff out of which is extracted possible shape and meaning.

I encourage clients with recurring patterns or emotional snares that limit their lives to explore the roots of these patterns in past-life stories. We go back to the very first time they experienced the pattern or emotion. Their unconscious mind makes up a story about what happened, and that story can provide insights that help reframe the experience. Is the story truly a memory of a past life? Perhaps. But it doesn't really matter. It is only an archetype, a myth, a context for the person to gain new learning and insights. Since life is a point of view, past-life dramas give leverage for us to change our view. It is like installing an update in your computer—it applies to all lives after it, including the present. It changes the person at a deep visceral level.

While it is not within the scope of this book to teach past-life regression, those who wish to explore can do so by using their imaginations and following their sensations, or by working with a past-life therapist to guide them.

The following two stories give examples of the experience of accessing past lives.

My teacher guided me into a past-life experience by first having me identify a feeling, which was slight sadness. I amplified that feeling, expanding it more and more, amplifying it 200 percent, until I began getting images. The nuances of sadness deepened into a devastating feeling of loss. I realized I was no longer in my body. I was trying to get back to it, but I couldn't. I seemed to have been a large man covered by a mudslide, and all I could see were my Cossack boots sticking out of the mud. The desolation of having lost my body was the worst loss I could ever imagine, and I sobbed uncontrollably. My teacher asked me if I could go to the light. When I looked, there *was* a light in the sky, but I couldn't leave my body. Finally, he persuaded me to move toward the light. I glanced back at the body, but it was no more significant to me than a twig or a pebble; it held absolutely no emotional attachment for me. I was pulled up toward the light by a sense of anticipation that I had important things to do.

The past-life experience of dying could have been traumatic; I was fortunate that my teacher first guided me into it and then helped me move on. As I reflected on this, I realized the death of one life was nothing for me to fear. I seemed to be able to transition to new life and new purpose by focusing on the light rather than on the loss. Whether this is true or not, who knows? But the strange story that emerged from my unconscious gives me a sense of calm.

A friend described another method and gave an example:

"The technique I learned for past-life recall begins with a quiet, calm state [there are thousands of books and teachers who can tell you how to achieve this]. When you're relaxed and receptive, imagine, or perhaps experience, that you're leaving your body and rising up above the earth, which is spinning backward through the years. You drop down into another time, of your conscious or unconscious choosing. Take in the details of your surroundings and your body to determine where you are and who you are. Learn your situation. When you're satisfied, rise up and immediately drop down into the most meaningful day of this life, and learn what you can from it. At this point, you can visit as many other days as you like or go directly to the day of your death. Again, observe and learn. Before you die, leave your body, harvest the most important lessons of that lifetime, and ask how they apply to your life in the present day. Finally, lift above the spinning earth and return to yourself now.

"Here is a past life I recalled. My memories of that distant time are as vivid as the memories of experiences, not of daydreams.

"Epidauros in Greece was the site of the greatest healing center, or Asclepion, in the ancient world. In the present, I was there with a tour group, and it made sense to guide myself into a past life there. I barely had time to lift above the earth and look down before I was in the body of a young man, very pleased with myself to have been chosen to lecture on philosophy to the visitors who came for healing (a sound, informed, agile mind was considered a necessity for the health of the whole being). I moved on to my next episode, where I was in a field, scythe in hand, harvesting grain, bare to the waist, sweating and reveling in the pleasure of working hard. From this bright afternoon, I absorbed the lesson that mind and body, to say nothing of emotions and spirit, must exist in harmony, and even though I loved my intellect, there was more to me. On my last day, I found myself lying beside a mountain trail. I had fallen from my mule, whom I could smell and hear munching grass nearby. My neck was broken. Rising above, I looked down with love and compassion on my dying self and rejoiced with an almost effervescent gratitude that I had served Asklepios, the healer-god, and lived such a happy and loving life."

Whether you believe or disbelieve in the existence of past lives, I go for the practical. If past lives are useful, then I am interested. Whether past lives are fact or fiction, here are some ways to gain from their exploration:

- They may give you insight into skills, life patterns, or core beliefs latent in you. You see yourself in a larger context, a bigger picture. Like the whole iceberg, with the tip above the surface and the massive mountain of ice below, past lives encompass greater definition and potentiality of both skills and issues.

- They may provide an avenue for the unconscious mind to give you metaphors for resolving issues or expanding consciousness. Like the stories with morals or values we tell children, these past-life stories can take us beyond the local self.
- You can reinvent yourself in a larger context—your way. We are constantly bombarded by stories that depict reality for us and sell others' values. If we reach into ourselves for these stories rather than getting them from movies, TV shows, novels, politicians, and the like, we are taking charge of our own evolution. If we don't like the story, we can change it, because, after all, it is *our* story.

It is up for grabs as to how you use past-life metaphors to expand your present-life potential.

Treasure Hunt

Have you felt an unexplained affinity to a person, a place, or a skill (musical instrument, sport, art, culture)?

Do you believe past lives are real?

Have you had an experience that seems to be of a past life or heard someone relate such an experience?

Have you had a past-life reading or therapy?

Drawing on your personal experiences and beliefs, design a way to use what you uncover as a metaphor or seed to expand your current-life potential. One way is to go back to an imaginal past life where you had a unique skill or ability. Download that experience and bring it forward to your present life to increase your current abilities.

Chapter 26

Ancestral Connection

Wisdom lies deep in the vaults of our brains passed on
aeons ago by our ancestors.[112]

—Bryan

He threw bits of bones and things onto the mat and talked about my
life from patterns that only he could discern. He said I was being
guided and helped in my work by a great-aunt on my father's side. He
instructed me to meditate to get her name and then to give a dinner
party for all my ancestors.

I left this session with the wizened, gifted African healer P.
H. Mntshali as amazed by the accuracy of his reading as by the
strangeness of it all to my Western mind. However, I dutifully
meditated for my great-aunt's name and learned that it was Emily.
That evening I placed food in as many tiny saucers as my kitchen
table would hold, sending a mental invitation to all my ancestors,
including my deceased dad, to join me at a feast in their honor. As I
nibbled on the food, I acknowledged my genealogical lineage.

I was startled out of this by the phone. It was my mom, who
never calls me unless it is very important, and my sister. They were
thinking of me and decided to chat. Laughing, I told them I was
in the middle of a dinner party for our ancestors, and Dad said to
give her his love. My mom wasn't at all surprised. When I asked if
Dad had ever mentioned an Emily in his family tree, she checked
his family Bible and reported a great-aunt Emily among the dozen

or so names recorded! That seemed well beyond coincidence. I felt suffused with a loving, warm glow of support and belonging.

Valuing connections to ancestors as an essential part of life has always played a central role in indigenous and ancient cultures, among them Native American, Chinese, and Hawaiian. In fact, most of these cultures consider pleasing and honoring one's ancestors to be an integral part of daily ritual. "All my relations" is a common greeting used when entering a sweat lodge. Before modern times, when Hawaiians chanted their genealogy, they would not take a breath in the middle, because to break the lineage with a breath would be dishonorable. A study of the Hawaiian language discloses a deeply ingrained belief that everything is related. Even the most mundane things have a higher connection, which is why the Hawaiians did not separate the everyday from the spiritual. An integral part of fishing, for example, was connecting with the presiding deities of the elements, the weather patterns, the ocean, and the fish.[113]

That reminds me of a story. A guy walks into a pet store and sees two TV monitors, each with a video of a fish swimming around. When one fish turns, so does the other, in exact synchrony! Amazed, the guy asks how the two fish do that. Well, there were two cameras showing the same fish from different angles. The moral is, we may look different, but we're all one fish!

Treasure Hunt

To connect with your ancestors, start by gathering everything you know about your cultural and biological heritage. Where did your ancestors live? What were their beliefs, their way of life, their skills and affinities?

Describe what you feel particularly drawn to in such areas as music, dance, art, and religion.

What do you know of your grandparents and great-grandparents, either personally or through family stories? Which were you particularly close to or fond of? What characteristics or personality traits did you inherit from them?

Often the spirit of an ancestor from farther back than you can remember may have been your guardian through life. You may want to design a series of meditations to invite that person to become known to you. You can carry on an ongoing dialogue with them, asking for their advice and intercession.

Section VI

Engaging Subtler Resources

In section V you practiced the following things:

- playing with different perspectives to view an issue
- harnessing nth factor energies like the placebo effect
- increasing the flow of giving and receiving as a spiritual practice
- exploring possible past lives for influencing patterns
- connecting with your ancestors.

In section VI you will learn to use even subtler resources for your change work, like nature, color, and light.

- Looking to nature and the cosmos for instructive patterns can lead to developing rituals that will restore your personal ecology and the global ecology.
- Colors have a direct influence on your entire being—your biological clock, your moods, your sleep, and your energy levels. Experimenting with the effects of color on you personally can make deep and subtle changes.

- Your body is light-sensitive. You can suffer from mal-illumination. Further explore your relationship with light and color.
- The last chapter uses the Hawaiian analogy of the body as a gourd filled with light. Upsets, conflicts, and worries add pebbles to your gourd, blocking the light. Changing within gives you tools to keep your gourd free from the stones that block your inner light.

Chapter 27

Nature as Teacher, Nature as Template

The more our world functions like this natural world,
the more likely we are to be accepted on this home that
is ours, but not ours alone.[114]

—Janine Benyus

We are the acorns through which flow the patterns of mighty oak
trees. As a seed, each of us grows into the manifested existence of
the mind knowing itself. Through us, the world knows itself. We are
the flow-through for star stuff and galaxies.

Nature teaches us how to be. Any solution can be found by
observing the patterns of nature. The farther from nature we stray,
the more out of balance we become. Imagine a completely synthetic,
man-made world where everything, including our food, housing,
and clothing, is inorganic and synthetic. No wood, no sweet peaches,
no cotton or silk. Imagine living in a bubble where artificial light
simulates natural sunlight and where recycled air is regulated to
maintain the proper percentages of oxygen, carbon dioxide, and
nitrogen. What would our quality of life be? How long would we
last?

Everything is interconnected. Biodiversity is essential for the
planet. And yet our planet is currently experiencing the worst die-
off of species since the loss of the dinosaurs sixty-five million years
ago. Extinction naturally occurs at a rate of about one to five species
per year. But we are losing species at one thousand to ten thousand
times that rate, with dozens going extinct every day. This could lead

to 30–50 percent of all species heading to extinction by midcentury. Unlike past mass extinctions, caused by natural events like asteroid strikes, volcanic eruptions, and cyclic climate shifts, the current crisis is almost entirely caused by human activities, primarily from habitat loss and global warming. Because the rate of change in our biosphere is increasing, and because every species' extinction potentially leads to the extinction of others bound to it in a complex ecological web, the number of extinctions is likely to snowball in the coming decades as ecosystems unravel. So why would we care about the extinction of so many species?

> Whether we and our politicians know it or not, Nature is party to all our deals and decisions, and she has more votes, a longer memory, and a sterner sense of justice than we do.[115]
>
> —Wendell Berry

At least 40 percent of the world's economy and 80 percent of necessities for the poor are derived from biological resources. In addition, the richer the diversity of life, the greater the opportunity for medical discoveries, economic development, and adaptive responses to such challenges as climate change. Sectors dependent on genetic resources include pharmaceuticals—25-50 percent, $640 billion in 2006; biotechnology—$70 billion from public companies alone; and agriculture—$30 billion. Nearly 90 percent of known human diseases can be treated with prescription drugs derived from nature. Half of all written prescriptions could not be filled without the cornucopia of gifts from the stunning biodiversity of the wild natural world. Half of the top ten prescription drugs in the United States are of animal, plant, or microorganism origin. One-third of all our food—fruits and vegetables—would not exist without pollinators visiting flowers. But honeybees, the primary species that fertilizes food-producing plants, have suffered dramatic declines in recent years, mostly from afflictions introduced by humans.

Many of our recent innovations and solutions look to nature for their source. The technique, called biomimicry, takes a design challenge and finds an ecosystem that's already solved it and tries to emulate it. Wikipedia describes biomimicry as "an approach to innovation that seeks sustainable solutions to human challenges by emulating nature's time-tested patterns and strategies." It is the imitation of the models, systems, and elements of nature for the purpose of solving complex human problems. Below are some innovations that have come from mimicking nature:

Efficiency of motion. A technology modeled on humpback whales' incredible dexterity in turning tight circles and sharp angles by using flippers with large, irregular tubercles across their leading edges has been applied to increase the efficiency of wind turbines. It is used on the bottoms of boats to improve their speed and efficiency. It has enormous potential applications to the performance and safety of airplanes and fans and the like.

Improved surgeries. Needles and surgical penetration tools designed like the stingers of mosquitoes and certain wasps cause less pain. They allow surgeons to insert their tools more delicately and deeply, leaving, for example, little or no damage in brain surgeries.

Faster, quieter trains. The Shinkansen Bullet Train in Japan had a huge noise problem, which was solved by modeling the front end of the train after the beaks of kingfishers, which dive into bodies of water with very little splash. The reengineering resulted not only in a quieter train but also in 15 percent less electricity usage even while the train was traveling 10 percent faster.

More efficient building design. An office building in Zimbabwe has an internal climate control system modeled on termite mounds.

Velcro. One of the best known and most commercially used examples of biomimicry is Velcro, invented by Swiss engineer George de Mestral. He was inspired by burrs that attached to his dog's fur with tiny hooks.

Bacteria repellant. Sharkskin stays remarkably clear of algae and bacteria because of its design. Mimicking the shark, boats have decreased their drag to keep their bottoms clear of algae and microorganisms. Now surface materials using this design to repel bacteria are found in hospitals, kitchens, and public bathrooms.

Water extraction from air. A Namibian beetle collects fog water droplets by means of bumps on its back. A Dew Bank Bottle designed in Seoul imitates this water-collection system to catch morning dew in a drinking bottle.

Reduced power consumption. Regen Energy uses a beehive pattern to turn its company's power-sucking machines into a network that balances its loads for maximum efficiency.

Superstrong adhesive! Gecko tape mimics geckos' ability to scamper up and down smooth walls and move upside down across ceilings using the millions of tiny hairs, setae, that have an attraction that disappears when the direction is changed. The adhesive Geckskin is so strong that an index-sized card can hold up to seven hundred pounds.

Preservation at high temperatures. The resilient microanimal desert tardigrade can survive extreme dehydration for more than a century, preserving its DNA, RNA, and proteins until revived with water. Biomatrica has used this technology to preserve vaccines for long periods and in high temperatures.

One way we can heal ourselves and our increasingly polluted environment and overused natural resources is to listen to the indigenous people. I asked Loretta Cook, Oglala Lakota from Pine Ridge Indian Reservation in South Dakota, to share her thoughts on this subject. Starting with the big picture and the interconnection of everything, she said everybody has a magic. *Wakantanka* (Great Mystery) is magic—and not just everyday magic, but serious, big, sacred magic. "We accept life in its entirety," she said, "connecting with all of the winged, connecting with all of the four-leggeds, connecting with the minerals. In this way we express our big magic by connecting with all of nature."[116]

Our current lifestyles are by and large devoid of ritual and ceremony, which used to feed our souls and connect us with the larger stuff of life, the flow-through of star stuff and galaxies.

Ceremonies can bring about changes through symbolic enactments, as powerful as prayer and focused thought-form. One example of a healing nature ritual is to ceremonially plant trees native to your area; they hold the spiritual power and depth that fast-growing crops do not have. In California the tree might be the redwood. On the island of Molokai, Kumu John Kaimikaua started a project to plant Lehua seedlings in an area long ago stripped of its sacred Lehua forests. In a ritual dedicated to restoring some of the original foliage, the planting was accompanied by prayer, hula dances, and chanting, performed by schoolchildren and *hula halau* (schools). Today the seedlings are growing into a successful reforestation project.[117]

Loretta Cook says that her people are taught to take only as much as they need, so there will always be enough for everybody in the world, and always to look out for each other. Because we have not done that, it will take many, many years to restore and heal our natural resources. We need to be extra mindful to help conserve and to make up for our past indulgences and overusage.[118] Small rituals may not make much difference right away, but symbolically they become powerful trim tabs. A trim tab is the tiny rudder that turns the big rudder that turns the huge ocean liner. Buckminster Fuller adopted the term as a metaphor for an individual's ability to affect a larger organism. A ritual you might try is to turn off the water while you brush your teeth, rather than letting it run. Each tiny act becomes a prayer ritual to offset our world of convenience.

Treasure Hunt

Connecting with the Rhythms of Nature

How aware are you of the cycles of the moon, if it's waxing or waning, full or dark? Since the moon has a powerful pull on the waters, it affects our bodies the way it affects the ocean tides,. Do you know where the sun rises and sets in summer versus winter? What starry constellations do you regularly track, like the Big Dipper or Orion? How much do you sleep each night? Does it vary depending on the season or the weather? Do sun flares or full moons affect you? Have you dowsed the energy and tracked the ley lines in your house and property?[119]

Ritual

You can devise a ritual for cleansing your land and home and bringing in blessings and positive energy. While you may include chanting, prayer, Reiki, and drumming, remember that a ritual has everything to do with intention. You can ask that negative energy go elsewhere, that restless entities find another home or return to the light. Imbue your property with the energies you want, like peace, abundance, safety, and love. Then close your ritual ceremony by asking that it be so.

Indebtedness to Nature

What products are you using that were developed by mimicking nature? How can biomimicry help you solve problems? Which of your medicines and drugs were found in nature? For example, rapamycin is a bacterial by-product discovered in the soil on Easter Island. It is already used with stents and in transplant patients to prevent organ rejection. Captopril was developed from the venom of the fer-de-lance viper found in the tropics; it treats hypertension and high blood pressure. When you consider things you take for granted, your indebtedness to nature will surprise you.

Chapter 28

I'm in the Mood for Color

Red is such an interesting color to correlate with emotion, because it's on both ends of the spectrum. On one end you have happiness, falling in love, infatuation with someone, passion, all that. On the other end, you've got obsession, jealousy, danger, fear, anger and frustration.[120]

—Taylor Swift

Colors are more than aesthetics or personal preference. They directly influence our entire being. Colors are not only able to clear destructive patterns, they can also turn on fresh qualities of intelligence. Color instantly makes deep and subtle changes directly in the information stored in our light bodies and our thoughts, memories, feelings, and experiences.

Here are some of my clients' experiences with colored lights:

- "My chronic lower back pain disappeared with twenty seconds of yellow light on my forehead. Another time I got rid of a sore throat with one minute of blue light."
- "My daughter's grades improved and her reading ability increased from not being able to read a whole book to majoring in English in college, after twenty light treatments using a Lumatron[121] light machine."
- Two teen subjects stopped having violent temper tantrums, and their college grades went from Cs and Ds to As and Bs after the same treatments.

Colors have different properties and psychological effects. Red, orange, and yellow are outer-directed, yang, day colors, warming and stimulating. Blue, green, and violet are inner-directed, cool, mellowing colors. Blue may be relaxing to one person and depressing to another. One person may feel anxious with red, while another may be uplifted and motivated.

In winter a red jacket will give a warmer sensation than a blue one. We eat faster in a restaurant with orange decor (check the fast-food places), while we tend to linger and relax when surrounded by green. Yellow stimulates thinking. We sleep more deeply in blue sheets. Blue hospital rooms promote calm and healing following major surgery. Blue rooms are sometimes used to quiet violent inmates in mental institutions.[122]

To experiment with the effects of color, any medium is fair game. Immerse yourself in the experience of a single color, say, green. Eat only green foods, wear green, surround yourself with green, wear green-tinted glasses. Using gels or plastic colored sheets over a light or flashlight, you can shine a green light on your body or illuminate a room. Do this for a day to discover what effects that color has on you—how you feel, what emotions come up, and where in your body you experience the color. If it had a voice, what would it say to you? Notice if it makes you feel uplifted or earthbound, restful or anxious. Notice your breathing for depth or shallowness. Notice if it sedates or tonifies, warms or cools. Beyond merely liking or disliking a color, you can explore the effect it has on your energy and physical body, your psyche and your light body.

Treasure Hunt

To take the suggestions above to a deeper, more personal level, experiment with enhancing not only your moods and energy but also your overall health and well-being with colors. Keep a journal of the results as a scientific record.

Chapter 29

Light as Medicine for Your Body

Coauthored by Martha Rigney[123]

> There is a relationship between the light that we let into our vision and the light of consciousness. ... David Bohm once said that all matter is frozen light. This simply means that everything in our reality, from matter to consciousness, is light. We also need to keep in mind that light is a nonmaterial reality, and since light makes up our reality this truly gives us something to consider when we start expanding the way we see our world.[124]
>
> —Jacob Liberman

Not only do our eyes see light, our whole body is light-sensitive. Our skin absorbs light and acts as a prism to break out the different colors, which become information to the body. Blind people can accurately detect colors with their hands. We absorb the light around us as much as the air we breathe, and our body responds to different color frequencies.

Just as we can suffer from malnutrition, we can have mal-illumination, as color seems to be a necessary nutrient to the brain and body. Color and light control our biological clock, mood, sleep and wakefulness, subjective energy levels, and appetite for carbohydrates. The autonomic nervous system that controls heart rate, lungs, intestines, glands, and other organs is influenced by the nerve endings in the skin. Color wavelength frequencies penetrate the capillaries and are absorbed by the blood, creating wide changes in the body's metabolic, endocrine, emotional, and vitality functions.

In the late 1800s, Dinshah Ghadiali and Dr. Edwin Babbitt successfully pioneered applying colored lights to the body to cure diseases and treat conditions such as burns, candida, incontinence, teething, tendonitis, insect bites, and phobias, to name a few. Others who contributed to color therapeutics include Rudolph Steiner, Sir Isaac Newton, Robert Bunsen, and Sir William Crookes. With the advent of antibiotics, these colored-light treatments were actively discouraged. Dinshah was prosecuted in federal court for fraud, the US Post Office would not send his material, and his work was destroyed in a fire at his institute. As late as 1985, the Federal Drug Administration (FDA) prevented the Dinshah Health Society from selling its color projectors, contending they were medical devices. Yet Dinshah was astoundingly successful. In one of his most famous cases he healed, with only a fraction of the usual scar tissue, a child so severely burned that he was considered hopeless for skin graft. Dinshah maintained that the potency of light and color far exceeds that of drugs and serums.[125]

Recent studies confirm that color has healing properties. A standard procedure in hospital neonatal units for the underdeveloped livers of newborns is blue bili lights, accelerating the conversion of bilirubin to bile, proving that light has a direct effect on the liver and kidneys. A study showed that blue light on an area affected by rheumatoid arthritis can reduce pain. Protection from red or yellow, by green-lens glasses, for example, can diminish tremor, torticollis, and some conditions in Parkinson's. Light therapies have had documented successes in the treatment of seasonal affective disorders (SAD), sleep disorders, depressive states, dyslexia, PMS, phobias, carbohydrate craving, obesity, and headaches. In students treated with light therapy, researchers have reported longer attention span, increased visual and auditory memory, greater emotional well-being, reduced hyperactivity and tension, and improved ability to handle criticism.[126]

Now, color is making a resurgence, this time with new technology. Studies have revealed that our bodies emit colored electromagnetic energy. Our cells act as tiny photoelectric batteries. Not only do cells share chemical reactions, they also gather light and send it to other cells. This light network is one of the main communication systems in the body.[127]

Since the body is made up of color, and communication within it is in living color, color can be an important therapeutic modality. Peter Mandel of Germany developed colorpuncture to apply the right frequency of color to specific points in the body, releasing energetic information that travels instantly through the body, affecting the most subtle functioning of cells, organs, and minds. It works directly on information stored in our light bodies as well as on thoughts, memories, feelings, and experiences, instantly making deep and subtle changes. Light and color may be our rainbow bridge to enhancing our health.

Treasure Hunt

Personalize your relationship with different colors. Take an inventory of the colors around you—your walls, your furniture, your rugs. What colors dominate your wardrobe? What tones dominate your everyday life?

What effects do different colors have on you? Using scarves, cloths, or tissue paper, cover yourself with different colors. Or shine a light through colored plastic or cellophane onto your body. If you treat your body with bright red, does your breath become more shallow or deeper, are you calmer or tenser, and does your pulse quicken or slow? With blue, do you relax or perhaps become despondent and blue? Whichever way, relax into the colors to become aware of how they make you feel. Take the time necessary to allow your body to give you its reactions. Based on what you observe, how can you use color to enhance your quality of life?

Chapter 30

Your Vessel of Light

Blessed are the cracked, for they shall let in the light.[128]
—Groucho Marx

Ancient Hawaiians saw the body as a gourd filled with light. Their concerns, upsets, and worries put pebbles and stones in their bowl, weighing it down and blocking the light. Because the body vessel is meant to contain light, energy, pure potential, creativity, and joy, it is important to clean it regularly of the baggage that impedes and clogs these things. The ancient Hawaiians knew this and regularly turned their vessel over, dumping out whatever was blocking their light and joyous expression.

Hawaiians use many techniques to release what weighs them down or blocks their light. Here are some ways that they *huli* or turn over their vessels of light to clean them.

Take care how you talk to and about yourself and others. We beat ourselves up with something like, "Oh, that was stupid! You dummy, why don't you watch what you're doing?" Many self-conversations drag us farther into negative, destructive self-talk. A first step in emptying your bowl is to talk respectfully and positively to yourself. Extending that courtesy to others also helps keep the bowl clean.

Resolve issues quickly so they don't build up. Lingering irritations, grudges, and unspoken resentments put pebbles in your bowl and block your light. Better to talk about them and let them go rather than carry around a whole bowlful. Think about a time when you wanted to clear up a disagreement with a friend or loved one, and suddenly they brought up old resentments about something you did last week, last year, five years ago, or even when you were a kid. They never dumped out their bowl! They had been carrying around those resentments like pebbles that blocked not only their light but also how they saw you.

Many Hawaiians regularly use their breath to clear their minds, release upsets, and center and calm themselves. The *ha* breath is in a 1:2 ratio, with the out breath twice as long: breathe in for a count of four and out for a count of eight. Use the exhale breath to release tensions and emotions along with the stale air. In hula class, if students came in distracted or upset, the *kumu* teacher would tell them to take some deep *haaa* breaths (long exhale, making a sighing sound) before letting them join the class. And before a hula performance, the dancers all breathe together in this slow, calming rhythm.

Avoid shame, embarrassment, guilt, and resentment. By being mindful of their connection to others and to their environment, the Hawaiians honor their *kuleana*, duty or responsibility. By keeping these connections respectful and clean, they avoid shame and embarrassment from disrespectful actions. They believe that one should caretake these connections with humbleness, whether to the land, the fish, the plants, or the elders. Disrespect brings repercussions and unwanted outcomes, like a poor crop, no fish in the nets, or shameful feelings that precipitate poor health. Not respecting the environment can mean it will respond in a negative way. If this seems foreign, remember you are glimpsing not just the theory but the experience of another culture with subtle but powerful differences in values!

The concept of our bodies giving off light is not limited to the Hawaiians. Many paintings portray saints, holy people, Jesus, Buddha, and the like with halos of light around their heads. Kirlian photography measures the light corona of energy emitted from an energized object such as a person's hand or a leaf. To end on a light note, they say angels fly because they take themselves lightly! The less cluttered we keep our vessels of light, the greater conductors of light we become.

Treasure Hunt

Contemplate the following quotation and write what it means to you personally:

> We shape clay into a pot, but it is the emptiness inside that holds whatever we want.[129]
>
> —Lao Tzu

Conclusion

If you've read *Change Within, Change the World*, it probably means you want something different, whether an expansion of consciousness or a shift in perspective. Shifts come in many different ways and at many different speeds. After years of meditation and prayer, a monk became enlightened. An ordinary man was struck by lightning and became a shamanic healer. In Lewis Carroll's book *Alice in Wonderland*, Alice fell down a rabbit hole and found her world turned topsy-turvy. Albert Einstein got his most famous insight, the theory of relativity, in a dream.[130]

The point is, change comes in different ways for different people.

However you interacted with this book, take a moment to acknowledge the changes you made. What kinds of changes were they—gradual, contemplative, or in a flash of insight? Were they physical, psychological, mythic or spiritual, mental or emotional? Was it beliefs or values that changed? How will these changes manifest in your life? Honor your changes: the time you take to acknowledge and inventory your personal unique changes honors you and the time you took to process the information.

Your inner changes become your springboard to make changes in the external world. It's not the knowledge you acquire; it's what you *do* with it that's important.

> Don't fear the struggle; fear the feeling that makes you not want to partake in that struggle.[131]
> —Jenson Merrick

It's not easy to heal yourself. It takes work. Be honest about how you really feel. For you to love others, you need to first love yourself. Change within. Then change the world.

Endnotes

1   The book and DVDs are available at my website, changewithin.com.

2   Even though my topic is Change Within, I often feel that my writings are inspired by something outside myself. I call that source of inspiration the Muse. While the Greeks had as many as nine Muses, I believe their company has room for more, and I have welcomed the Muse of Writing, the Muse of Potentiality, and the Muse of Inner Truth. I like the sense that areas of endeavor are guided by aspects of the divine feminine. I honor and respect them all.

3   Attributed to Mahatma Gandhi, although there is no reliable documentary evidence.

4   Jean Houston, *Jump Time*, p. 11.

5   Ibid., p. 16.

6   James Baldwin, "As Much Truth as One Can Bear," *New York Times Book Review* (January 14, 1962).

7   Elisabet Sahtouris, "Touch the Future," accessed June 12, 2018. https://ttfuture.org/academy/elisabet-sahtouris/elisabet-sahtouris.

8   Ulrich J. Mohrhoff, "Evolution of Consciousness According to Jean Gebser," Sri Aurobindo International Center of Education, anti-matters.org/articles/74/public/74-67-1-PB.pdf.

9   Clare W. Graves, "The Never Ending Quest," accessed August 30, 2018. http://www.clarewgraves.com/theory_content/quotes.html.

10   Pierre Teilhard de Chardin, Jesuit priest, philosopher, paleontologist.

11   Pierre Teilhard de Chardin.

12   Pierre Teilhard de Chardin, *The Phenomenon of Man.*

13   Pierre Teilhard de Chardin.

14   Pierre Teilhard de Chardin.

15   Pierre Teilhard de Chardin.

16   See Fuller's works *Synergetics* and *Spaceship Earth.*

17   Rupert Sheldrake, www.mavericks.com/shell-int.htm.

18   Jose Arguelles, *Earth Ascending* and *The Mayan Factor.* He propounded his views in many radio broadcasts as well.

19   https://www.globalresearch.ca/mayan-prophesy-prepare-yourself-for-the-end-of-the-world-at-global-research/5316429.

20   Buckminster Fuller, *Beyond Civilization: Humanity's Next Great Adventures* (1999), Daniel Quinn, p. 137.

21   Frederic Laloux, *Reinventing Organizations: A Guide to Creating Organizations Inspired by the Next Stage of Human Consciousness* (Brussels: Nelson Parker, 2016), p. 90.

22   https://ttfuture.org/academy/elisabet-sahtouris/elisabet-sahtouris.

23   Elisabet Sahtouris and James E. Lovelock, *EarthDance: Living Systems in Evolution.*

24   Risk contagion is sometimes called the "domino effect." Like the plague, risks are interconnected. One risk can amplify the many others with which it interacts. The Global Risk Reports of the World Economic Forum for every year cited show maps demonstrating the ways a shock in a particular sector of an economy, or political situation, or environmental condition spreads out, both domestically and internationally, to affect other sectors and magnify the risks.

Many academics and analysts see global market interdependence as one of the primary causes of risk contagion. Examples come from recent financial crises. The crisis of 2008 mowed down banks in the United States and Europe with equal abandon. When the East Asian oil crisis in 1997 was at its peak, interest rates in Hong Kong rose and fell drastically, transmitting volatility as far away as Argentina, Chile, and Mexico.

The 2017 Atlantic hurricane season provides another example. In August, when category 4 Hurricane Harvey made landfall in the Houston–Beaumont, Texas, area, floods, closed roads, power outages, property destruction, and other calamities shut down the energy infrastructure along the Gulf of Mexico. Energy production in the region declined by 21 percent and refining capacity dropped by 13 percent, causing energy prices in Europe and Asia to shoot sky-high.

25 "Global Risks Report 2018," 13th ed., World Economic Forum, p. 6.

26 Ibid., p. 16.

27 Paul Hawken, quoted in Brandon Gaille, https://brandongaille.com/39-wonderful-paul-hawken-quotes/.

28 For a notion of what has gone into my research, I refer you to the bibliography.

29 "What Is a Cooperative?," Coop International Cooperative Alliance, https://ica.coop/en/what-co-operative.

30 Ibid.

31 "List of Cooperatives," Wikipedia, last modified May 31, 2018, https://en.wikipedia.org/wiki/List_of_cooperatives.

32 "What Is a Cooperative?," Coop International Cooperative Alliance.

33 Ibid.

34 Ibid.

35 Rupert Sheldrake, author, researcher.

36 Hafiz, *The Gift: Poems by Hafiz, the Great Sufi Master.*

37 *RPI News*, Rensselaer Polytechnic Institute.

38 Attributed to Margaret Mead, cultural anthropologist (original source uncertain).

39 Viktor E. Frankl, neurologist, psychiatrist, Holocaust survivor.

40 Eric Butterworth, "The Law of Visualization," *Unity: A Positive Path for Spiritual Living*, http://www.unity.org/resources/articles/law-visualization.

41 Iain McGilchrist, *The Master and His Emissary: The Divided Brain and the Making of the Western World*, p. 15.

42 Osho, mystic, guru, spiritual teacher.

43 Arundhati Roy, from the speech "Confronting Empire," presented at the World Social Forum in Porto Allegre, January 28, 2003.

44 James Carroll, scholar, columnist.

45 Ria Baeck and Helen Titchen Beeth, "Collective Presencing: Embracing a New Paradigm," *Kosmos Journal for Global Transformation*, http://www.kosmosjournal.org/article/collective-presencing-embracing-a-new-paradigm/.

46 Jean Houston, "Dr. Jean Houston," Rising Women Rising World, http://risingwomenrisingworld.com/portfolio-items/dr-jean-houston/.

47 Mahatma Gandhi, statesman, spiritual and political leader.

48 Samuel Johnson, author, linguist, lexicographer.

49 Osho.

50 Roger McGough, "What the Little Girl Did," *The Mersey Sound*, p. 76.

51 William Shakespeare, *Hamlet*, Act II, Scene 2, lines 251–252.

52 Writing in a stream-of-consciousness way: writing unstructured, unedited thoughts, observations, and feelings as they occur to you; like brainstorming.

53 Emily Dickinson, poet.

54 Eleanor Roosevelt, social activist, first lady.

55 Jevon Dängeli describes this in presupposition #11 on his website, https://jevondangeli.com/. Other useful sources for this concept are Dängeli's *User Manual for Your Mind and Life* and *The User's Manual for the Brain* by Bob G. Bodenhamer and L. Michael Hall.

56 Osho.

57 T. F. Hodges, teacher, blogger, author of *From Within I Rise*.

58 The title of this section is a paraphrase of "The Ground on Which I Stand," the name August Wilson gave his famous declaration of his position on black theater and the common values of American theater. http://aas.princeton.edu/blog/publication/thegroundonwhichistand/.

59 Jarod Kintz, author, *This Book Is NOT FOR SALE*.

60 You can patch in several ways. Use an eye patch. Or buy two pairs of sunglasses at the dollar store and pop out the right lens of one and the left lens of the other. Tape a piece of construction paper over the remaining lenses. Or use a small sleeve (baby sock with ends cut off) to slide left to right on your existing glasses.

61 John O'Donohue, poet, philosopher, lecturer, author of *Anam Cara*.

62 J. K. Rowling, author of the *Harry Potter* series.

63 Roman Payne, poet, novelist, author of *The Wanderess*.

64 Rick Ingrasci, cofounder of Hollyhock Institute and StoryDome Project.

65 Hank Wesselman, *The Bowl of Light: Ancestral Wisdom from a Hawaiian Shaman*, p. 144.

66 Stephen Covey, author of *The Seven Habits of Highly Effective People*.

67 NeuroLinguistic Programming (NLP) is like having an operating manual for your brain. Formulated in the 1970s by John Grinder and Richard Bandler, it is a series of techniques and methodologies to show how the brain stores, processes, and retrieves information, and it helps one understand how those brain functions affect feelings, emotions, and consequent behaviors. A key element of the NLP techniques is modeling people of excellence to extract the patterns and strategies they use to attain such high skill levels.

68 Kami Garcia, author of *Beautiful Darkness*.

69 William Shakespeare, *Hamlet*, Act III, Scene 4, line 230.

70 Bruce Lipton, quoted in "How Cell Memories Are Formed and Their Impact on Your Health," Mind's Ease, http://mindsease.com.au/how-cell-memories-are-formed-their-impact-on-your-health/.

71 Bruce Lipton, *The Biology of Belief*.

72 Lewis Carroll, Chapter VI, "Pig and Pepper," *Alice's Adventures in Wonderland*.

73 J. K. Rowling, *Harry Potter and the Chamber of Secrets*.

74 Colleen Hoover, *Hopeless*.

75 Jarod Kintz, *This Book Title Is Invisible*.

76 Roy Disney, executive.

77 Stephen R. Covey, *The Seven Habits of Highly Effective People: Powerful Lessons in Personal Change*.

78   Thich Nhat Hanh, *No Mud, No Lotus: The Art of Transforming Suffering.*

79   Wendell Berry, *The Country of Marriage.*

80   Albert Einstein, theoretical physicist, Nobel Prize winner.

81   Jean Houston, lecture notes, West Coast Mystery School, 2005.

82   Lewis Carroll, Chapter V, "Wool and Water," *Through the Looking Glass and What Alice Found There.*

83   Cited in many sources, including *Multiple Personality Disorder from the Inside Out,* edited by Barry M. Cohen, Esther Giller, and Lynn W.

84   Arjun Walia, "Scientific Studies Show Meditators Collapsing Quantum Systems at a Distance," *Collective Evolution* (May 2014), https://www.collective-evolution.com/2014/05/01/scientific-study-shows-meditators-collapsing-quantum-systems-at-a-distance/. Dean Radin, Leena Michel, James Johnston, and Arnaud Delorme, "Psychophysical Interactions with a Double-Slit Interference Pattern," *Physics Essays* (December 2013): 553–66, https://www.aapsglobal.com/wp-content/uploads/2018/04/Radin-Psychophysical-interactions-with-a-double-slit-interference-pattern.pdf. Dennis Relojo, "Link between Mind and Quantum Physics Confirmed," *Psychreg Journal of Psychology* (August 2017), https://www.psychreg.org/link-mind-quantum-physics/.

85   Albert Einstein.

86   Developed by Jean Houston, the energetic wall of time is a process in which the participants travel by means of their imaginations back in time to a specific event. They reimagine it, that is, construct an alternate memory, a different way the event might have gone that would have produced a more positive outcome in the present. Many people find that a new element has entered the memory or that present-day effects of the event have lessened or even disappeared, as Dr. Houston shows in her example. She introduced this process at her Mystery Schools in 2005.

87 Tao Te Ching.

88 Mark Twain, humorist, novelist, writer, lecturer.

89 First Corinthians 13:11, King James Version, National Publishing Company, p. 1195.

90 Stephen Wolinsky, *Trances People Live.*

91 Lailah Gifty Akita, *Pearls of Wisdom: Great Mind.*

92 Any system that oscillates back and forth has a point at which it changes direction. A pendulum swings in one direction and then reverses and swings in the other. Movement in one direction appears to be at rest before reversing. Heisenberg's uncertainty principle states that we can know momentum or position; if we're certain about one, we can't know the other. If we know momentum, we don't know position, and vice versa. At the point where a pendulum changes direction, it is at rest, and we know its velocity is zero. But that means we cannot know its whereabouts. It can be just about anywhere in the universe. It instantly disappears in all directions and then comes back to resume its oscillation. The split-instant rest point is significant because constant rest would equate to nonaliveness. Source: Itzak Bentov, chapter 3, in *Stalking the Wild Pendulum: On the Mechanics of Consciousness.*

93 David Allen, productivity consultant.

94 Friedrich Nietzsche, philosopher.

95 Deepak Chopra, medical doctor, author of *The Seven Spiritual Laws of Success.*

96 Jean Houston, "The Jumps of Jump Time," Jean Houston Foundation, http://jeanhoustonfoundation.org/resources/the-jumps-of-jump-time-2/.

97 Louise Hay's book *Heal Your Body—The Mental Causes for Physical Illness and the Metaphysical Way to Overcome Them* is an excellent reference for this.

98 Christiane Northrup, MD, women's health expert, author of *Women's Bodies, Women's Wisdom*.

99 In "Discovering the Capacity of Human Memory," *Brain and Mind* (2003), Wang et al. reported that human memory has been discovered to have a capacity of about 10 to the power of 8,432 memory bits, each of which represents a possible connection pathway between neurons via synapses.

100 Michael Talbot, *The Holographic Universe*; Sheila Ostrander and Lynn Shroader, *Psychic Discoveries Behind the Iron Curtain*.

101 Dalai Lama, head of state and spiritual leader of the people of Tibet; winner of the Nobel Peace Prize.

102 Vincent van Gogh, letter to Anthon van Rappard (August 18, 1885).

103 Neale Donald Walsch, author of *Conversations with God*.

104 Gary Zukav, *The Dancing Wu Li Masters*.

105 https://home.cern/topics/higgs-boson.

106 Candace Pert, *Molecules of Emotion*.

107 John Sarno, *Healing Back Pain—The Mind-Body Connection*.

108 Valerie Hunt, *Infinite Mind: Science of the Human Vibrations of Consciousness*.

109 Kirlian photography is an array of techniques for capturing images of the electrical coronal discharges radiated by a creature (plant or animal) and reflecting the subject's internal state. A broad range of frequencies, transmitted at fifty thousand volts, resonate with the body's biological and energetic exchange. Many call the resulting image the aura. Energy practitioners use the information for diagnosing and healing emotional and physical conditions. https://en.wikipedia.org/wiki/Kirlian_photography.

110 Michael Talbot, *The Holographic Universe*.

111 Gautama Buddha, teacher and religious leader.

112 Bryan, "3833," Board of Wisdom, https://www.boardowisdom.com.

113 In *The Bowl of Light*, Hank Wesselman describes the kahuna Hale Makua's deeply personal, reverent connection with his ancestors, so foreign to Western ways. If you're interested in delving into your ancestral bonds, this book is well worth reading.

114 Janine Benyus, chapter 1, "Echoing Nature: Why Biomimicry Now?" in *Biomimicry: Innovation Inspired by Nature*, Biomimicry Institute, https://biomimicry.org/janine-benyus/first-chapter-biomimicry-innovation-inspired-nature/.

115 Wendell Berry, endorsement statement for *The Dying of the Trees* (1997) by Charles E. Little.

116 Loretta Cook, private communication.

117 Personal communication.

118 Personal communication.

119 Dowsing is used to locate the earth's energy lines, sometimes called ley lines, as well as underground water, pipes, electrical lines, and mineral deposits. Dowsers usually employ a pair of L-shaped metal rods, which you can make out of wire coat hangers or copper wires. Your intention is most important—to communicate with the earth, which you do by concentrating on your specific question. Walk the area you are exploring, with your hands loosely grasping the short legs of the *L*. Keep the long legs parallel to the ground, pointing straight ahead in a neutral position. When you step into the flow of the energy lines, the rods will open like double doors, then return to neutral. They will point three times in the direction of the energy, each time going back to neutral. As you continue to walk, the rods will repeat this action, always pointing three times in the direction of the flow. To map the area, note where the energy lines occur. Many thanks to dowsing practitioner Alison May for this information.

120 Taylor Swift, singer-songwriter.

121 Jane Battenberg, "The Effects of the Lumatron on Visual Field and Learning and Emotional Abilities," unpublished study, 1992.

122 Studies, references, and sources are cited in *Eye Yoga* (Battenberg and Rigney), chapter 18, "Effects from Visual Intake of Light," pp. 183–93; and *Light: Medicine of the Future* (Jacob Liberman), chapter 8, "Light, Color & Learning," pp. 101–107.

123 This chapter was developed from "I'm In the Mood for Color" by Dr. Jane Battenberg and Martha M. Rigney, *The Voice* 4, no. 1 (May–June 2004): 6.

124 Jacob Liberman, quoted in Lotus Guide, "Interview with Dr. Jacob Liberman," http://lotusguide.com/interview-with-dr-jacob-liberman/.

125 Darius Dinshah, *Let There Be Light*.

126 Studies, references, and sources are cited in *Eye Yoga* (Battenberg and Rigney), chapter 18, "Effects from Visual Intake of Light," pp. 183–93.

127 http://www.greenmedinfo.com/blog/biophotons-human-body-emits-communicates-and-made-light and others.

128 Groucho Marx, comedian, actor.

129 Lao Tzu, Tao Te Ching, chapter 11.

130 http://www.dreaminterpretation-dictionary.com/famous-dreams-albert-einstein.html. http://www.world-of-lucid-dreaming.com/10-dreams-that-changed-the-course-of-human-history.html.

131 Jenson Merrick, private communication.

Glossary

aura: The invisible yet distinct atmosphere or quality that surrounds and is emanated by a person, thing, or place.

autism: Also known as autism spectrum disorder, a range of conditions characterized by challenges with social skills, intellectual disability, speech, repetitive behaviors, and nonverbal communication. It typically appears between ages two and three.

bilirubin: A reddish-yellow water-insoluble pigment formed by the breakdown of heme. It is secreted by liver cells into bile and occurs in blood and urine, especially in diseased states.

biodiversity: An environment as indicated in the numbers of different species of plants and animals.

biomimicry: An approach to innovation that seeks sustainable solutions to human problems by emulating nature's patterns and strategies.

biosphere: The regions of the surface, atmosphere, and hydrosphere of the earth occupied by living organisms.

blue bili light: An ultraviolet-emitting light source that is used to care for infants with neonatal jaundice. It is a type of phototherapy that helps to convert bilirubin into a form that can be detoxified by the liver.

bodhi: The tree under which the Buddha was sitting when he attained enlightenment. The words *bodhi* and *Buddha* both are derived from "awakening." The sacred fig tree at Bodh Gaya, India, is said to be a direct descendant of the Buddha's tree, and saplings from it have been planted all over the world, including in Thousand Oaks, California, and Honolulu. Prayer beads made of sacred fig wood are considered especially holy because of their association with the Buddha.

brain neuroplasticity: Cellular regeneration, the brain's ability throughout life to reorganize itself by forming new neural connections. Neuroplasticity allows the neurons (nerve cells) in the brain to compensate for injury and disease and to adjust their activities in response to new situations or changes in the environment.

CERN (*Conseil européen pour la recherche nucléaire*), the European Organization for Nuclear Research, is located in Meyrin, near Geneva, Switzerland. The largest particle physics laboratory in the world, it provides the infrastructure required for high-energy research. Among the achievements of physicists associated with CERN are the confirmation of the existence of the Higgs boson and many Nobel Prizes for Physics. Much of CERN's work involves the Large Hadron Collider, a worldwide, cooperative project. The immense quantities of data it generates are streamed around the world. The World Wide Web was invented by a CERN employee.

deep implicate-order intelligence: Physicist David Bohm theorized three orders of reality. Deepest is *intelligence,* from which is derived the *implicate order,* in which every element contains information about every other element. The implicate gives form and organization to the manifest—*explicate*—reality that we experience and is enfolded in it. The three levels exist in a closed, continuous loop. Bohm offers this analogy: the explicate order is the images, the implicate order organizes them into a game, and intelligence plays the game.

ecosystems: A biological community of interacting organisms and their physical environment.

emoji: A small digital image or icon used in electronic communication to express an idea or emotion. Similar but less sophisticated and flexible is the emoticon, which is created on a standard keyboard: :) for example (colon and right parenthesis coming together to make a sideways smiling face).

fractals: The word was coined by mathematician Benoît Mandelbrot. They are infinitely complex, self-similar patterns that repeat across different scales, revealing more and more details. Robert L. Devaney explained thus: "Think of trees, with their trunks, large limbs, smaller limbs, branches, smaller branches, twigs, and so on" (http://bigthink.com/articles/mathematician-benoit-mandelbrot). The term *fractal* has been extended to describe other repeating patterns, such as stock prices and the rise and fall of water levels in a river.

ha breath: Ha, meaning breath, refers to the sacred breath of life that enlivens every human being and unites all as one in spirit.

harmonic convergence: The name given to an event that took place August 16–17, 1987, when one of the world's first globally synchronized meditations occurred. The event was defined by Jose Arguelles as "the point at which the counter-spin of history finally comes to a momentary halt, and the still imperceptible spin of post-history commences." It was an announcement of the forthcoming end of time as we know it and a preparation to move from third-dimensionality of space into fourth-dimensional reality of time.

Higgs boson: An elementary particle with zero spin and large mass in the standard model of particle physics. In 1964, François Englert and Peter Higgs presented separate papers predicting the existence of this fundamental particle, which was confirmed in 2012.

holographic: A three-dimensional image reproduced from a pattern of interference produced by a split coherent beam of radiation, such as a laser.

homeopathic: A system of medical practice that treats a disease by the administration of minute doses of a remedy that would in larger amounts produce in healthy people symptoms similar to those of the disease.

huli: Means "turn" in Hawaiian.

Huna: A Hawaiian word adopted by Max Freedom Long in 1936 to describe his theory of metaphysics. The Huna was originally called Ho'omana, meaning "to empower" or "empowerment."

hypnotherapy: The practice of hypnosis for therapeutic purposes. The hypnotic trance state is a remarkably flexible tool for solving mental and physical health problems.

imaginal: Coined by philosopher Henry Corbin, who envisioned a three-part universe—spiritual, material, and imaginal—where "matter is spiritualized and spirit is materialized." Imaginal describes much more than the creations of mere imagination; it has come to refer to a high order of ideas from universal consciousness (called higher genius, God, platonic, divine, optimal template, mythic resonance) emerging in space and time.

kinesthetic: From the Greeks words *kinein* (move) and *aisthesis* (sensation). Describes sensory experiences derived from movement and physical sensations. Kinesthetic learning comes through such feelings as a sense of body position, muscle movement, and weight. Dancing is a kinesthetic art form.

kuleana: Responsibility or duty (Hawaiian).

kumu: Teacher, one who has achieved the highest level of expertise in an area such as hula, chanting, or fishing (Hawaiian).

Lehua: A tree indigenous to the Hawaiian Islands.

lomilomi: "Massage therapist," "Hawaiian massage." The Hawaiian word *lomi* means "to knead like a contented cat." When the word is doubled for emphasis, *lomilomi*, it refers to the spiritual shift caused by healing.

Lumatron: A neurophotonic device that emits a high optical-quality light with a variable flicker rate that passes wavelengths of visible light through the eye, increasing the amount of electrical energy flowing through the brain. Studies by the inventor John Downing, OD, PhD, Jacob Liberman, OD, PhD, and author of this book, Jane Battenberg, MA, DCH, among others, show that Lumatron treatments stimulate better brain function, balance brain–body chemistry, and enhance intellectual capacity as well as emotional well-being. It provides light as a nutrient to the brain as vitamins provide nutrients to the body. Results of the studies can be found in *Eye Yoga*, pp. 183–93.

mal-illumination: An environmental condition characterized by the absence of full-spectrum light.

Maya calendar: A system of interweaving circular calendars recording everyday, historical, and mythic happenings and predicting future events, dating back at least to the fifth century BCE. It was used in pre-Columbian Mesoamerica and is still in use in many modern communities in the Guatemalan highlands and some regions of Mexico. The creators used their advanced knowledge of astronomy and mathematics to devise the calendar.

mechanistic Newtonian physics: In 1687, Sir Isaac Newton proposed that the world is mechanical, operating with mathematical precision and predictable phenomena. According to Newton's laws and his theory of a clockwork universe, God established creation and the cosmos as a perfect machine governed by the laws of physics, where matter was viewed as passive and was moved and controlled by "active principles," in which he included gravity as well as "that which causes fermentation."

metaverse: A virtual-reality space in which the user can interact with a computer-generated environment and other users.

mind map: An easy way to brainstorm thoughts organically, without worrying about order and structure. A nonlinear graphical layout builds an intuitive framework about a central subject, representing visually how tasks, words, and concepts are linked to the main subject and to each other.

mogul field: A ski run with complex and inconsistent terrain.

Multilateral Agreement on Investment: A draft agreement negotiated between members of the Organization for Economic Cooperation (OECD), 1995–1998. While some provisions would have established a secure environment for international investments, it was widely regarded as biased toward the interests of rich countries at the expense of poorer nations and encroaching upon national sovereignty. For the first time, the internet was influential in generating opposition. NGOs pressured France to withdraw in 1998, and the agreement failed.

multiple personalities disorder (MPD): A condition in which two or more distinct identities, or personality states, are present in, and alternatively take control of, an individual.

neocortex: A part of the cerebral cortex concerned with sight and hearing in mammals, regarded as the most recently evolved part of the cortex.

noosphere: A term meaning "mind sphere" introduced by Pierre Teilhard de Chardin in *Cosmogenesis* (1922). Teilhard conceived a "thinking layer" encircling the earth that has been expanding and maturing as life grows in complexity—therefore, it is a part of nature. It continues to expand as language, thought, and consciousness develop, as the human race's self-knowledge and awareness of its relationship to the planet increase. He believed the noosphere will emerge fully at a peak mystical movement he called "the Omega Point" and will be the next phase of human evolution.

past-life regression: A therapeutic technique used for accessing and reexperiencing past lives directly. It is a branch of hypnotherapy.

pheromones: A chemical substance that is produced by an animal, especially a mammal or insect, that serves as a stimulus to other individuals of the same species for one or more behavioral responses. It is also called ectohormone.

placebo: A placebo appears to be a medical treatment but in fact contains no active substance meant to affect health. Some individuals respond to a placebo as they would to a treatment, either with improved symptoms or with side effect. These responses are called the "placebo effect." https://www.webmd.com/pain-management/what-is-the-placebo-effect#1.

The effect seems to demonstrate that the healing comes from the mind, from believing in the treatment. Recent studies have gone beyond simple belief, however, to demonstrate that the mind is indeed a healer, but people can be aware they are receiving a placebo—a saline solution, a sugar pill, a smear of Vaseline—rather than the "real" thing and nevertheless receive the benefits of the medical treatment. Neuroscientist, chiropractor, and author Dr. Joe Dispenza is a leader in the field of rewiring the brain to increase health.

placenta previa: A condition in which the placenta partially or wholly blocks the neck of the uterus, interfering with the normal delivery of a baby.

quantum energy field: The theoretical framework for constructing quantum mechanical models of subatomic particles in particle physics and quasiparticles in condensed matter physics.

quantum physics: The branch of physics concerned with quantum theory.

seasonal affective disorders (SAD): A type of depression related to changes in seasons.

shamanic death and rebirth experience: The death of an old way of being making way for the birth of a new one, generally while remaining alive on this plane, although some individuals do indeed die. In many cultures, people deliberately seek the experience through ritual or intense spiritual practices. For others, the passage is involuntary, without planning or preparation, precipitated by a traumatic event such as an illness, an injury, or a life crisis that awakens them to a deeper life.

sixth global extinction biologically: Otherwise referred to as the Holocene extinction. The ongoing extinction of species during the present Holocene epoch, mainly as a result of human activity.

stream of consciousness: A term introduced by William James in his work "Principles of Psychology" in 1890, whereby someone writes or orally expresses thoughts as they occur, rather than in a structured way. Free association of words or ideas.

tardigrade: A minute, water-dwelling microanimal capable of surviving extreme conditions. Also called a water bear.

telepathy: From the Greek word *tele* meaning distant and *pathos* meaning strong feeling, passion, affliction. Coined in 1881 by Frederick W. H. Myers, founder of the Society for Psychic Research. The communication of thoughts or ideas by means other than the known senses.

tipping point: The point at which a series of small changes or incidents accumulate, becoming significant enough to cause larger, more important change.

torticollis: A condition in which the head becomes persistently turned to one side, often associated with painful muscle spasms.

Treaty of Rome: The Treaty of Rome or Rome Statute established the International Criminal Court (ICC) in 1998. Under the statute, the ICC prosecutes the four international crimes of genocide, crimes against humanity, war crimes, and crimes of aggression, which are subject to no statute of limitations, but only when a state is unable or unwilling to do so. Not even a head of state is immune from prosecution. The United States, Russia, Israel, and Sudan signed the treaty but have since dissolved their legal obligations—that is, have withdrawn their signatures; 123 states remain parties to the statute.

Vedic science: The term for modern attempts to systemize the ancient scientific thought found in early Indian scriptures, especially the Vedas.

virtual energy: In quantum physics, a very short-lived, unobservable quantum state. In many quantum processes a virtual state is an intermediate state, sometimes described as "imaginary" in a multistep process that mediates forbidden transitions (those with a low probability of occurring).

Selected Bibliography and Suggested Readings

Abbey, Edward. *The Journey Home*. New York: Plume, 1997.

Arbinger Institute. *An Anatomy of Peace: Resolving the Heart of Conflict*. Berkeley: Berrett Koehler, 2006.

Arguelles, Jose. *Earth Ascending*. Santa Fe: Bear & Company, 1988.

_____. *The Mayan Factor: Path Beyond Technology*. Santa Fe: Bear & Company, 1987.

_____. *Manifesto for the Noosphere: The Next Stage in the Evolution of Human Consciousness*. Berkeley: Evolver Edition, 2011.

Baker, Dean. *False Profits: Recovering from the Bubble Economy*. Washington, DC: PoliPoint, 2016.

Bar-Cohen, Yoseph, ed. *Biomimetics: Nature-Based Innovation*. Boca Raton: CRC Press, 2011.

Baring, Anne. *The Dream of the Cosmos: A Quest for the Soul*. Dorset, United Kingdom: Archive Publishing, 2013.

Battenberg, Jane, and Martha Rigney. *Eye Yoga: How you see is how you think*. Minneapolis: Langdon Street Press, 2010.

_____. "I'm In the Mood for Color," *The Voice of Orange County* (May–June 2004). Costa Mesa: In Living Color.

Beck, Don Edward, and Christopher Cowan. *Spiral Dynamics: Mastering Values, Leadership, and Change.* Wylmington, Hants, United Kingdom: Spartan Press Ltd., 1996.

Bentov, Itzak. *Stalking the Wild Pendulum: On the Mechanics of Consciousness.* Rochester, VT: Destiny Books, 1998.

Benyus, Janine. *Biomimicry: Innovation Inspired by Nature.* New York: Harper Collins, 2004.

Birx, H. James. *Interpreting Evolution: Darwin and Teilhard de Chardin.* New York: Prometheus Press, 1991.

Bodenhamer, Bob G., and L. Michael Hall. *The User's Manual for the Brain.* Carmarthen, United Kingdom: Crown House, 2001.

Boone, J. Allen. *Kinship with All Life.* San Francisco: Harper Press, 1954.

Briggs, John, and F. David Peat. *Turbulent Mirror.* New York: Harper Row, 1990.

Capra, Fritjof, and Pierre Luigi Luisi. *The Systems View of Life: A Unifying Vision.* Cambridge, England: Cambridge University Press, 2014.

Capra, Fritjof. *The Tao of Physics: An Exploration of the Parallels between Modern Physics and Eastern Mysticism.* Boston: Shambhala Publications, 1975.

———. *The Turning Point: Science, Society, and the Rising Culture.* New York: Simon & Schuster, 1982.

Chomsky, Noam, and Peter Hutchinson. *Requiem for the American Dream: The 10 Principles of Concentration of Wealth & Power.* New York: Seven Stories Press, 2017.

Chomsky, Noam, and Arthur Naiman, eds. *How the World Works.* New York: Soft Skull Press, 2011.

Chomsky, Noam, and C. J. Polychroniou. *Optimism Over Despair: On Capitalism, Empire, and Social Change.* Chicago: Haymarket Books, 2017.

Chopra, Deepak. *Quantum Healing: Exploring the Frontiers of Body/ Mind Medicine.* New York: Penguin Random House, 1989.

Cohen, Barry M., Esther Giller, and Lynn W., eds. *Multiple Personality Disorder from the Inside Out.* Brooklandville, MD: Sidran Press, 1991.

Dängeli, Jevon. *User Manual for Your Mind and Life.* 2012. nlpwizardry.com.

Dawlabani, Said Elias, and Don E. Beck. *MEMEonmics: The Next Generation Economic System.* New York: Select Books, 2013.

Dionne, E. J. Jr. *Our Divided Political Heart: The Battle for American the Idea in an Age of Discontent.* New York: Bloomsbury, 2013.

Dinshah, Darius. *Let There Be Light.* Malaga, NJ: Dinshah Health Society, 1985.

Dispenza, Joe. *Breaking the Habit of Being Yourself: How to Lose Your Mind and Create a New One.* Carlsbad: Hay House, 2012.

_____. *Evolve Your Brain: The Science of Changing Your Mind.* Deerfield Beach, FL: Health Communications, 2008.

_____. *You Are the Placebo: Making Your Mind Matter.* Carlsbad: Hay House, 2014.

Dychwald, Ken. *Body-Mind.* Los Angeles: Jeremy Tarcher, 1986.

Eisner, Riane. *The Chalice and the Blade: Our History, Our Future.* New York: HarperCollins, 1987.

Fritz, Robert. *The Path of Least Resistance: Learning to Become the Creative Force in Your Own Life.* Boston: MA Press, 1984.

Fuller, Buckminster. *Critical Path.* New York: St. Martin's Press, 1981.

_____. *Earth, Inc.* New York: Anchor Press, 1973.

_____. *Synergetics: Explorations in the Geometry of Thinking.* New York: Macmillan, 1975.

Gebser, Jean. *The-Ever Present Origin.* Ohio University Press, 1985.

Geer, Richard, and Jules Corriere. *Story Bridge: From Alienation to Community Action.* San Bernardino: Performance Press, 2014.

Gladwell, Malcolm. *The Tipping Point: How Little Things Can Make a Big Difference.* New York: Little, Brown, and Company, 2000.

Graves, Clare W. *Levels of Human Existence.* Santa Barbara: ECLET Publishing, 2002.

_____. *The Never-Ending Quest.* Santa Barbara: ECLET Publishing, 2008.

Greenfield, Susan. *Mind Change: How Digital Technologies Are Leaving Their Marks on Our Brains.* New York: Random House, 2015.

Grof, Stanislav. *The Adventure of Self-Discovery.* New York: New York State University Press, 1998.

_____. *The Cosmic Game: Explorations of the Frontiers of Human Consciousness*. New York: State University of New York Press, 1998.

_____. *Psychology of the Future*. New York: State University of New York Press, 2000.

Grof, Stanislav, and Hal Zina Bennett. *The Holotropic Mind*. New York: HarperCollins, 2002.

Hanh, Thich Nhat. *Being Peace*. Berkeley: Parallax Press, 1987.

_____. *Peace Is Every Step*. New York: Bantam Books, Doubleday, 1992.

Hawken, Paul. *Blessed Unrest: How the Largest Movement in the World Came into Being and Why No One Saw It Coming*. London: Penguin Books, 2007.

Hay, Louise. *Heal Your Body*. Los Angeles: Hay House, 1976.

Hedges, Chris. *The World as It Is: Dispatches on the Myth of Human Progress*. Washington, DC: Public Affairs Publishing, 2013.

Herman, Edward S. *Manufacturing Consent: The Political Economy of Mass Media*. New York: Pantheon, 2002.

Houston, Jean. *Jump Time: Shaping Your Future in a World of Radical Change*. New York: Tarcher Putnam, 2000.

_____. *Life Force*. New York: Dell, 1980.

_____. *A Passion for the Possible: A Guide to Realizing Your True Potential*. San Francisco: Harper, 1997.

_____. *The Possible Human*. New York: Tarcher Putnam, 1982.

Hunt, Valerie. *Infinite Mind: Science of the Human Vibrations of Consciousness.* Malibu: Malibu Publishing Company, 1996.

Hutchison, Michael. *Megabrain: New Tools and Techniques for Brain Growth and Mind Expansion.* New York: Ballantine, 1991.

Jeffers, Susan. *Feel the Fear and Do It Anyway.* New York: Nook Books, 1987.

_____. *Embracing Uncertainty: Breakthrough Methods for Achieving Peace of Mind When Facing the Unknown.* New York: St. Martin's Press, 2004.

Jung, Carl Gustav. *Man and His Symbols.* New York: Random House, 1964.

_____. *Symbols of Transformation.* New York: Routledge & Kegan Paul Ltd., 1956.

Keyes, Ken. *The Hundredth Monkey.* Los Angeles: De Voss & Company, 1983.

Klein, Naomi. *No Is Not Enough: Resisting Trump's Shock Politics and Winning the World We Need.* New York: Haymarket Books, 2017.

_____. *The Shock Doctrine: The Rise of Disaster Capitalism.* New York: Metropolitan Books, Henry Holt & Company, 2007.

_____. *This Changes Everything: Capitalism vs. the Climate.* New York: Simon & Schuster, 2015.

King, Serge Kahili. *Urban Shaman: Mastering Your Hidden Self.* New York: Simon & Schuster, 1990.

King, Ursula. *Spirit of Fire: The Life and Vision of Pierre Teilhard de Chardin.* New York: Maryknoll, 2015.

Korten, David. *The Great Turning: From Empire to Earth Community.* San Francisco: Berrett-Koehler, 2017.

_____. *Change the Story, Change the Future: A Living Economy for a Living Earth.* San Francisco: Berrett-Koehler, 2015.

Krishnamurti, J., and David Bohm. *The Ending of Time: Where Philosophy and Physics Meet.* New York: Harper Row, 1977.

Kolbert, Elizabeth. *Field Notes from a Catastrophe: Man, Nature, and Climate Change.* New York: Bloomsbury USA, 2017.

_____. *The Sixth Extinction: An Unnatural History.* New York: Henry Holt & Company, 2015.

Laborde, Genie Z. *Influencing with Integrity: Management Skills for Communication and Negotiation.* Palo Alto: Syntony, 1987.

Laloux, Frederic, and Ken Wilber. *Reinventing Organizations: A Guide to Creating Organizations Inspired by the Next Stage of Human Consciousness.* Brussels: Nelson Parker, 2014.

Liberman, Jacob. *Light: Medicine of the Future.* Santa Fe: Bear and Company, 1991.

Lipton, Bruce. *The Biology of Belief: Unleashing the Power of Consciousness, Matter, and Miracles.* Los Angeles: Hay House, 2016.

_____. *Spontaneous Evolution: Our Positive Future (and a Way to Get There from Here).* Los Angeles: Hay House, 2009.

_____. *The Wisdom of Your Cells: How Your Beliefs Control Your Biology.* Audio CD. Los Angeles: Sounds True, 2006.

Lovelock, James. *Gaia: A New Look at Life on Earth.* Oxford, England: Landmark Press, 2007.

_____. *The Revenge of Gaia: Earth's Climate Crisis & The Fate of Humanity*. London: Penguin, 2007.

_____. *A Rough Ride to the Future*. New York: The Overlook Press, Peter Mayer Publishing Inc., 2015.

Lovins, Amory B., L. Hunter Lovins, and Paul Hawken. *Natural Capitalism: Creating the Next Industrial Revolution*. Denver: Rocky Mountain Press, 2017.

Macy, Joanna. *Despair and Personal Power in the Nuclear Age*. San Francisco: New Society Press, 2012.

_____. *Greening of the Self*. London: Penguin Random House, 2013.

_____. *World as Lover, World as Self*. Berkeley: Parallax Press, 2003.

Mandell, Peter. *The Practical Compendium of Colorpuncture*. London: 1986.

Mayer, Jane. *Dark Money: The Hidden History of the Billionaires Behind the Rise of the Radical Right*. New York: Doubleday, 2016.

McGilchrist, Ian. *The Master and His Emissary: The Divided Brain and the Making of the Western World*. Boston: Yale University Press, 2010.

McKibben, Bill. *Deep Economy: The Wealth of Communities and the Durable Future*. New York: Henry Holt & Company, 2017.

McTaggart, Lynne. *The Field: The Quest for the Secret Force of the Universe*. New York: HarperCollins, 2002.

_____. *The Intention Experiment: Using Your Thoughts to Change Your Life and the World.* New York: Free Press, 2007.

_____. *The Power of Eight: Harnessing the Miraculous Energies of a Small Group to Heal Others, Your Life, and the World.* New York: Atria Books, 2017.

O'Donohue, John. *Anam Cara: Spiritual Wisdom from the Celtic World.* London: Harper Collins, Perennial Press, 1998.

_____. *The Invisible Embrace: Beauty: Rediscovering the True Sources of Compassion, Serenity, and Hope.* London: First Perennial Publications, 2003.

Oreskes, Naomi, and Erik M. Conway. *The Collapse of Western Civilization: A View from the Future.* New York: Columbus University Press, 2014.

Ostrander, Sheila, and Lynn Schroeder. *Psychic Discoveries Behind the Iron Curtain.* Upper Saddle River, NJ: Prentice-Hall Trade, 1984.

Packer, George. *Interesting Times: Writings from a Turbulent Decade.* New York: Macmillan, 2014.

Passino, Kevin M. *Biomimicry for Optimization, Control, and Automation.* London: Springer Press, 2004.

Pert, Candace. *Molecules of Emotions: Why You Feel the Way You Feel: The Science Behind Mind-Body Medicine.* New York: Scribner Press, 1997.

Prigogine, Ilya, and Isabelle Stengers. *Order Out of Chaos.* London: Bantam, 1984.

Radin, Dean, Leena Michel, James Johnston, and Arnaud Delorme. "Psychophysical Interactions with a Double-Slit Interference Pattern." *Physics Essays* (August 2017).

Reich, Robert B. *Saving Capitalism: For the Many, Not the Few.* New York: Henry Holt, 2016.

_____. *The Work of Nations: Preparing Ourselves for 21ˢᵗ Century Capitalism.* New York: Vintage, Random House, 1992.

Reiser, Oliver Leslie. *Cosmic Humanism.* Cambridge, MA: Schenkman, 1966.

Robertson, Brian J. *Holacracy: The New Management System for a Rapidly Changing World.* New York: Henry Holt, 2015.

Roy, Arundhati. *Capitalism: A Ghost Story.* Chicago: Haymarket Books, 2014.

_____. *The God of Small Things.* London: Random House, 1997.

_____. *The Greater Common Good.* Mumbai, India: India Book Distributors, Bombay Limited, 1997.

Russell, Peter. *Global Brain: Speculation on the Evolutionary Leap to Planetary Consciousness.* Los Angeles: J. P. Tarcher, 1982.

Sahtouris, Elisabet. *EarthDance: Living Systems in Evolution.* Lincoln, NE: iUniverse, 1996.

_____. *Gaia: The Human Journey from Chaos to Cosmos.* New York: Pocket Books, 2014.

Sarno, John. *Healing Back Pain: The Mind-Body Connection.* New York: Warner Books, 1991.

Schein, Edgar H. *Organizational Culture and Leadership*. Boston: Harvard Business Press, 2016.

Schumacher, E. F. *Small Is Beautiful: Economics as if People Mattered*. London: Blond and Briggs, 1973.

Sheldrake, Rupert. *A New Science of Life: The Hypothesis of Morphic Resonance*. Rochester, VT: Park Street Press, 1995

_____. *The Presence of the Past: Morphic Resonance and the Memory of Nature of Formative Causation*. Rochester, NY: Park Street Press, 2012.

_____. *The Rebirth of Nature: The Greening of Science and God*. New York: Bantam Books, 1997.

_____. *The Science Delusion: Freeing the Spirit of Inquiry*. London: Hodder and Stoughton, 2012.

Sheldrake, Rupert, Terence McKenna, and Ralph Abraham. *The Evolutionary Mind: Conversations on Science, Imagination, and Spirit*. Rhinebeck, NY: Monkfish, 2005.

_____. *The Evolutionary Mind: Trialogues at the Edge of the Unthinkable*. Rhinebeck, NY: Monkfish, 2005.

Sheldrake, Rupert, and Michael Shermer. *Arguing Science: A Dialogue on the Future of Science and Spirit*. Rhinebeck, NY: Monkfish, 2013.

Schonberger, Martin. *I Ching & the Genetic Code: The Hidden Key to Life*. Santa Fe: Aurora Press, 1973.

Steiner, Rudolf. *Freud, Jung, and Spiritual Psychology*. Barrington, MA: Anthroposophic Press, 1990.

————. *Start Now! A Book of Soul and Spiritual Exercises.* Barrington, MA: Steiner Press, 2004.

Talbot, Michael. *The Holographic Universe: The Revolutionary Theory of Reality.* New York: HarperCollins, 1991.

Teilhard de Chardin, Pierre. *The Divine Milieu.* New York: Harper Row, 1960.

————. *The Phenomenon of Man.* London: Penguin Random House, 2004.

————. *Toward the Future.* New York: Harcourt, 1973.

Tolle, Eckhart. *The Power of Now.* Vancouver: Namaste, 1999.

————. *A New Earth: Awakening to Your Life's Purpose.* New York: Penguin, 2005.

Walla, Arjun. "Scientific Studies Show Meditators Collapsing Quantum Systems at a Distance." *Collective Evolution* (May 2014).

Wang, Yingxu, Dong Liu, and Ying Wang. "Discovering the Capacity of Human Memory." *Brain and Mind* 4 (August 2003). http://www.cerebromente.org.br/home_i.htm.

Weber, Renée, ed. *Dialogues with Scientists and Sages: The Search for Unity.* London: Routledge and Kegan Paul, 1986.

Wesselman, Hank. *Awakening to the Spirit World: The Shamanic Path of Direct Revelation.* Boulder: Sounds True, 2010.

————. *The Bowl of Light.* Boulder: Sounds True, 2011.

Wilber, Ken. *A Brief History of Everything.* Boston: Shambala Press, 1996.

_____. _Integral Spirituality: A Startling New Role for Religion in the Modern and Postmodern World._ Boston: Integral Books, 2006.

_____. _No Boundary: Eastern and Western Approaches to Personal Growth._ Boston: New Science Library, 1979.

_____. _The Spectrum of Consciousness._ Wheaton, IL: Quest Books, 1993.

Wilber, Ken, ed. _The Holographic Paradigm and Other Paradoxes: Exploring the Leading Edge of Science._ Boulder: New Science Library, 1982.

Wolff, Richard. _Capitalism's Crisis Deepens: Essays on the Global Economic Meltdown._ Chicago: Haymarket Books, 2016.

_____. _Democracy at Work: A Cure for Capitalism._ Chicago: Haymarket Books, 2012.

Wolinsky, Stephen. _Trances People Live._ Ontario: Bramble Books, 1991.

_____. _Waking from the Trance._ Louisville, CO: Sounds True, 2002.

Yogananda, Paramahansa. _Autobiography of a Yogi._ Los Angeles: Self-Realization Fellowship, 1998.

Zdenek, Marilee. _Inventing the Future: Advances in Imagery That Can Change Your Life._ New York: McGraw Hill, 1987.

Zukav, Gary. _The Dancing Wu Li Masters._ New York: Bantam Books, 1997.

Index

A

Akita, Lailah Gifty 95, 168
Allen, David 103, 168
ancestors 93, 118, 139, 140, 141,
    143, 170
Arguelles, Jose 8, 12, 162, 175, 183
atemporal alternation 85

B

Babbitt, Edwin 154
Baeck, Ria 44, 164
Battenberg, Jane i, x, 48, 171,
    177, 183
Battenberg, Katherine 47
Beck, Don 13, 14, 18, 184
Beeth, Helen Titchen 44, 164
Benyus, Janine 145, 170, 184
Berry, Wendell 77, 146, 167, 170
bilirubin 154, 173
biodiversity 145, 146, 173
biological clock 143, 153
biomimicry 146, 147, 150, 170,
    173, 184, 191
biotechnology 146
blue bili lights 154, 173
Bohm, David 128, 153, 174, 189
Bryan 139, 170
Buddha 131, 157, 170, 174

Bunsen, Robert 154
Butterworth, Eric 40, 164

C

Captopril 150
carbohydrate craving 154
Carroll, James 43, 164
Carroll, Lewis 69, 80, 159,
    166, 167
change within i, xiii, xvi, xvii, xix,
    48, 117, 159, 161
chaos xix, 37, 128, 191, 192
choice, no choice 67
Chopra, Deepak 109, 168, 185
climate change xx, 23, 24, 146, 189
color 15, 62, 83, 84, 143, 144, 151,
    152, 153, 154, 155, 171,
    183, 184
colorpuncture 155, 190
competition i, xx, 13, 15, 19, 20, 21
complexification 8
consciousness xiii, xxi, 5, 6, 7, 8, 9,
    10, 12, 14, 16, 17, 18, 19, 46,
    75, 77, 134, 138, 153, 159,
    161, 162, 165, 168, 169, 176,
    179, 180, 183, 184, 187, 188,
    189, 192, 195
Cook, Loretta 148, 149, 170
Cooperative—stage

About the Author

Jane Rigney Battenberg, DCH, MA has more than twenty-five years of experience as a therapist and trainer, with a doctorate in clinical hypnotherapy, a master of arts degree in teaching, and certification as a master trainer of NeuroLinguistic Programming (NLP). She has studied such ancient arts as Huna, Reiki, and Lomilomi. Her earlier book, *Eye Yoga: How you see is how you think*, provides techniques for awakening deep brain capacities and improving eyesight. She gives workshops and counsels clients in the United States and Europe. Today Dr. Battenberg lives with her husband in Oregon. Learn more about her on her website **www.changewithin.com**.